SIGNS OF THE TIME

SIGNS OF THE TIME

Warning: Lukewarm Christianity Accepts Deception

R. C. JETTE

RESOURCE *Publications* · Eugene, Oregon

SIGNS OF THE TIME
Warning: Lukewarm Christianity Accepts Deception

All Scripture references are taken from the King James Version (KJV): KING JAMES VERSION, public domain.

Resource Publications
An Imprint of Wipf and Stock Publishers
199 W. 8th Ave., Suite 3
Eugene, OR 97401

www.wipfandstock.com

PAPERBACK ISBN: 978-1-7252-6333-8
HARDCOVER ISBN: 978-1-7252-6331-4
EBOOK ISBN: 978-1-7252-6332-1

Manufactured in the U.S.A.   02/03/20

First of all, this book is dedicated to
my Lord and Savior Jesus Christ who makes what seems
impossible possible through faith!

A special thanks is given to my husband, Paul,
who has encouraged me to keep writing. My daughter,
Dawn, who has helped free me up to write.

I also want to, with love, mention my son, PJ, his daughter,
Keira, my daughter, Christina, her sons, Andrew, Matthew,
Joshua and her daughter, Sarah, who is with the Lord. A warm
thanks to my cousins Susanna and Mike for their help.

My heartfelt thanks is given to Wipf and Stock Publishers
who have made my being a published author a reality and
have caused such gladness in my heart. Special mention must
be given to Matthew Wimer, Daniel Lanning, George Callihan,
Shannon Carter, and Savanah Landerholm to whom are more
appreciated than my words can express.

LET THE SCALES FALL

Let the scales fall,
Observe and perceive,
Comprehend the catastrophe,
Unrighteousness is out of control,
While man reaches to the moon,
The destruction of society,
Is multiplying all the dross,
Induced by selfishness, prejudice, hostility.

Let the scales fall,
Observe and perceive,
Comprehend the unrighteousness,
America's no longer One Nation Under God,
Lukewarm Christianity sits in churches,
Accepts the devil's deception,
While living a life of rebellion,
Beneath their mask of Christianity!

Contents

Introduction

THIS BOOK IS INTENDED for those who desire to get off the milk and partake of the strong meat of Scriptures. Let me illuminate that maturity will cost the denying of self.

I'm a firm believer in the truth that knowledge defeats destruction. Hosea 4:6 states: "My people are destroyed for lack of knowledge."

Knowledge is having an understanding, a comprehension, an awareness, or a realization of something. Where knowledge exists, there is the lack of ignorance or misconception. If God's soldiers are to overcome, we must be aware or conscious of the signs of the time. Only the faithful will uncover the signs hidden in Scripture. I mean, those who have learned to deny self and keep their bodies under submission to Christ.

This is not the time to be in ignorance about what's happening, lest we find ourselves oblivious of the signs happening before us. I am concerned about those who have claimed to no longer pay attention to the signs and are looking to the sky. This mentality is truly the pinnacle of chosen ignorance. In fact, it's playing into the devil's hands. A lack of awareness or ignoring what's happening, has God's soldiers ineffective. Such are no threat to the kingdom of Satan.

Soldier of God, this is not the time to avoid the signs, but to be even more conscious of what is occurring. The signs are, in fact, warnings or red flags that must be understood in the light of Scripture.

It's imperative that we learn to be aggressive in how we live and help others to be as assertive in the word of God. Too many have become lukewarm and are living a marshmallow Christianity that will not lead them or others to Heaven.

Listen to me, we cannot help others to overcome if we live as acquiescent, weak, obliging, complacent Christians. Sin is still as much sin as it was when Christ died for our sins.

I have learned through my years of ministry that too many are so concerned about being accepted by all, that they take no stand against sin, unrighteousness, unholiness, etc. We cannot be accepted by Christ and the world at the same time. We must choose to serve the Lord or others. If we serve people, we are not the servants of Christ.

Christ is not coming back for a lukewarm, compromising, deceived, or marshmallow bride, but a bride without spot or wrinkle. A bride who has correctly read and understood the signs as revealed in Scripture and has come through the refiner's fire as gold.

This book is to open our mind to see the whole of Scripture and not pull out our favorite verses, the belief we have been taught by our denomination, preacher, etc. It's time to reevaluate our beliefs. What do we believe? Why do we believe it? Were we taught it by man? Was it a Holy Spirit revelation? I urge all God's soldiers to study and to think more clearly about the word of God. Be led by the Holy Spirit and not what has been an accepted teaching.

Its focus is to illuminate the understanding of why it's imperative to beware of the signs of the time and the necessity of recognizing lukewarm Christianity. To read the signs with clarity will take self-denial. It will not be pleasant to those who desire itching ear preaching, and they will reject it's truth.

However, I'm not concerned about anything but projecting the truth to you who have ears to hear and will hear. Because you'll accept its truth, you'll receive the knowledge that will enable you to overcome. Yes, it will go against your flesh, and you will have a battle. However, your hunger for truth will allow you to receive Holy Spirit illumination to see you have been locked into false teaching and not the truth of the Scriptures. You will put your flesh under and persevere through to the end of this book, because you want to overcome and hear, "Well done, thou good and faithful servant."

To you who hunger for truth, read on faithful servant, and triumph as refined gold!

Chapter 1

Sign: False Indicators

In those days came John the Baptist, preaching in the wilderness of Judaea, And saying, Repent ye: for the kingdom of heaven is at hand. For this is he that was spoken of by the prophet Esaias, saying, The voice of one crying in the wilderness, Prepare ye the way of the Lord, make his paths straight. And the same John had his raiment of camel's hair, and a leathern girdle about his loins; and his meat was locusts and wild honey. Then went out to him Jerusalem, and all Judaea, and all the region round about Jordan, And were baptized of him in Jordan, confessing their sins. But when he saw many of the Pharisees and Sadducees come to his baptism, he said unto them, O generation of vipers, who hath warned you to flee from the wrath to come? Bring forth therefore fruits meet for repentance: And think not to say within yourselves, We have Abraham to our father: for I say unto you, that God is able of these stones to raise up children unto Abraham. And now also the axe is laid unto the root of the trees: therefore every tree which bringeth not forth good fruit is hewn down, and cast into the fire. I indeed baptize you with water unto repentance, but he that cometh after me is mightier than I, whose shoes I am not worthy to bear: he shall baptize you with the Holy Ghost, and with fire: Whose fan is in his hand, and he will thoroughly purge his floor, and gather his wheat into the garner, but he will burn up the chaff with unquenchable fire (Matthew 3:1–12).

In this chapter, we will look at two signs. One is the Star of Bethlehem and the other is the Hale-Bopp comet. However, the Star of Bethlehem, unlike the Hale-Bopp comet, is a celestial flare signaling where we can find the truth. Whereas, the comet was merely a scientific happening or false indicator.

The sad fact is the Hale-Bopp exposes or illustrates, all too clearly, the danger of believing or trusting false indicators. This book is meant to illuminate God's soldiers to false indicators being taught and believed in the church.

In July of 1995, two dedicated star observers turned their telescopes to the heavens and caught sight of a cosmic "trailer." Professional astronomer, Alan Hale, and amateur star gazer, Thomas Bopp, both noted and called in the first sightings of what appeared to be an unknown, unnamed comet.

It was, of course, duly labeled as comet Hale-Bopp. The preview show of Hale-Bopp was barely anything to excite most of us. It was something up there, visible only through a high-powered telescope.

But by March of 1997, when the Hale-Bopp comet "opened" to the general public, the show far exceeded all expectations. For weeks, the comet appeared bright and blazing in the northwest sector of the sky. Hale-Bopp was not a private showing to be viewed only by those with powerful telescopes.

It was a brilliant beacon we could all stand out on our porch and watch. Although we may never find the Big Dipper, or the less constellation Orion, we could authoritatively point Hale-Bopp out to others. Even the most astronomically challenged could look at it and comment knowingly to others, "Look, you can see its two tails. One is made of dust particles, the other is from water vaporizing."

Let's face it, when has a comet made so many of us who know very little about the cosmos sound so scientific literate?

But the comet's appearance not only encouraged scientific interest. It didn't just impress us with its brilliance. For many, Hale-Bopp was taken as a kind of cosmic signal-flare, a hidden sign of what was coming next. Across the Internet, Hale-Bopp was linked to UFO sightings and unexplained cosmic shadows.

The Heaven's Gate cult committing suicide, tragically, demonstrated how deadly it can be to misinterpret signs of any kind. For others, the relatively close approach (although it was still 122 million miles away) of such a massive hurling comet caused many to scurry and worry about how long planet Earth has until it's annihilated by one of these heavenly destroyers.

If our scientifically sophisticated, technologically advanced culture could get so enthusiastic about what Hale-Bopp was signaling to our planet, imagine how excited those first-century Jews, who were already expecting some sign from God, would have become at the sudden appearance of a "voice calling in the wilderness."

The crowds who flocked to him at the Jordan were like those standing on our front porches staring up at the night sky for a glimpse of Hale-Bopp. It was obvious that people wanted to see for themselves, to judge for themselves, what such a presence might mean.

John the Baptist saw himself and his ministry as an indicator of what was coming next. He confessed he was not the Christ, and he was quick to point out that while he was a signal, a sign pointing the way, he, himself, was not the source of the light (John 1:20, 23). John's purpose was to point toward who was coming next.

In mid-December, there is, of course, another bright star on our minds and on our horizon. In our minds, at Christmastime, is not the appearance of a grown Jesus asking to be baptized by John, but a single, shining star foretelling the birth of a tiny baby.

Like the Hale-Bopp, however, the Christmas star was also first noticed by just a few trained astronomers. The "Magi" kept careful watch on this peculiar star and began to follow its course across the sky. Gradually, the star grew brighter, more intense, and its light more focused, until it stopped in the sky directly over a small, trivial town called "Bethlehem."

No longer was this Star of Bethlehem noticed and followed by just the trained eyes of the Magi. Suddenly, it was an obvious presence to some shepherds in their fields. To all who looked heavenward, the Star of Bethlehem was a definite wonder that would raise questions as to its meaning.

But who would have thought such a brilliant heavenly beacon was necessary to shine on such a small and shabby stable. However, as bright and luminous as the star shone in the sky, it was dull in comparison to the Light that shone from that little baby in the manger. For in that manger, was He who created the very stars themselves.

The child was Jesus — whose birth was signaled by a star.

Jesus — who became our light, shining in the darkness.

Jesus — who is still the Morning Star, the Day Star, the Sun of Righteousness, and the Son of God.

The Prophets speak about Signs in the Heavens and Signs on Earth.

Today, many seek meaning for their lives in other places besides the heavens. Our bookstores are full of self-help books. Our television channels crammed with talk shows and commercials. Our mailboxes and emails are full of get-rich-quick schemes. Classrooms in schools and churches are filled in the evening with 12-step support groups. We have numerous ways on Earth to look for meaning, and for most that takes precedence over looking to the signs of the time.

This is a heartbreaking reality in the church. There are numerous signs or red flags pointing to the wreckage of Christianity. Yet, many are not looking to the Scriptures where what is occurring is forewarned.

Many believe man is God and makes or creates his own destiny. Sadly, this is rather correct. We do decide our own destiny. As soon as we reject Biblical Christianity's belief in a crucified Savior needed to save us from our sins, we have, of our own free-will, chosen our destiny to be eternity in Hell.

Too many claiming to be Christians are changing the signs to their own liking. We feel the old signs are archaic and limit our self-expression. The old signs are too confining, and the road is just too narrow and straight for comfort. So, changing the signs, allows for freedom of self-creativity.

The new signs, man-made signs, have no limitations to the indulging of Self Enterprise. With the majority following or looking for our own signs, our minds are not looking for any heavenly signs which tend to stifle self and its lust of the flesh, lust of the eyes, and the pride of life.

Yet, to the minds of the ancient Babylonian astrologers, who did watch the heavens for signs, a brilliant star in the heavens had meaning for them and for the world. And they sought to find out what it was and found their answer in Bethlehem.

At that time, there were people in ancient Israel who didn't always look heavenward for meaning, just as we have today. The Jewish faith was based on the law. There were those who found meaning for life in the scrolls, unconscious that they spoke about signs in the heavens.

Could it be that a star over Bethlehem, the scrolls of the law, and the prophets could all have the same purpose?

Without signs in the heavens or on Earth, we might have missed the miracle of the Messiah altogether. Jesus wasn't born in the public eye of a palace, nor was he born into the religious elite of Judaism. So, how was the world to find him without God posting some unmistakable and unforgettable signs, both in this world and in the heavens?

One such sign was the star in the heavens, a colossal event of great importance to those who studied the stars, such as the Zoroastrian astrologers in Babylon.

Another sign was John the Baptist, someone who had drawn a great deal of attention to himself by his lifestyle and by his preaching. Some who sought meaning for their lives were attracted to him, flocked to hear him, and to be baptized by him. Some in Jerusalem were as attracted to John the Baptist, as the wise men were attracted to that star.

Now, let's look at our Scripture text in Matthew 3:1–12. In verses 2–3, we see this is a prophetic voice with authority that rings out. John the Baptist, having only just begun to practice his "call" from God, wastes no time in exposing the rotten heart with its actions and attitudes that ran throughout the crowds gathering to hear him preach.

In fact, it seems rather odd for both Matthew chapter three and Luke chapter three to depict John the Baptist expressing harsh insults or rebukes to a crowd which had voluntarily gathered to hear him. A superficial look says if they were there, they already felt the tug of truth of John's message. Why else would they have come seeking a fresh start in this baptism of repentance?

For John to address such seekers with "you brood of vipers," and to hurl at them a heap of apocalyptic wrath of unquenchable fire, doesn't seem to be necessary with the crowd there to hear him.

Perhaps, not all of those who came seeking to hear him were moved by sincere repentance. Could it be that some in the crowd were merely seeking "insurance" against the "wrath to come" without repentance? His harsh words may well have been sparked by their unworthy motives.

Let's face it, how many are seeking for a way to escape the wrath to come without repentance. Many claiming to be Christians are flocking to the preachers and teachers having itching ears. We deceive ourselves into believing a simple prayer asking Jesus to be Savior guarantees entrance to Heaven without repentance or turning from sin.

But God knows the heart. John was led by God in his preaching. When we listen to our deceitful heart, we convince ourselves our motives are sincere and that's all that matters. However, God who sees what our heart is really about, knows we are only kidding ourselves.

When I first started to preach, I truly struggled with a message I was preparing. It seemed so harsh for my congregation. As a matter of fact, I thought my heart wasn't right with God. I felt they were going through so much with the storms and obstacles in their life, and I questioned how this message would help them. So, I prayed and asked the Lord to help me get my heart right.

He answered, "It's not YOUR heart I'm trying to get right. You see the façade they put on, I see their motives and intentions. I go home with them. I'm the one who knows and hears their every thought. I see their rebellion against my word. It's only truth that will set them free from their own deceitfulness. If truth is harsh, perhaps, you don't want to fulfill your call?"

Needless to say, that had the impact the Lord intended, and since that time, I don't concern myself with what I must preach or teach. I've learned not to be concerned if feelings get hurt. It's better to hurt weak sensibilities and help Christians to see the truth that will set free and inherit eternal life. After all, I'm here as his ambassador to Heaven.

I've learned from my years of experience in ministering that God sees the heart's thought before it's manifested in a life. Thus, when He tells me to hold a sign and flash it like a Neon Sign, I do it.

Not for my sake, but for those who have wrong thoughts festering in their hearts. God wants the fire of rebellion put out before it controls the whole being. It's not God's will for any to perish (2 Peter 3:9). He does everything to make the signs clear and noticeable to all who are willing to observe and obey them.

God's soldiers must realize that the whole word of God is full of signs for us to follow. It's our roadmap to Heaven. Yet, many are misinterpreting and are on the wrong path.

Let's face it, if we see a sign on the road "THE BRIDGE IS OUT: DO NOT ENTER" are we going to keep heading in that direction? Common sense says we won't.

Yet, how many read the signs in their personal roadmap, and ignore them. How many of us insist on being a hearer only of the word, and not do what it says to do?

Now, let's consider the text of this chapter. Is it not clearly a prophetic oracle revealing the hard and horrible truth about the wrath of God that awaits "vipers?"

According to the Baptist's testimony, there's only one way to avoid the coming judgment, and that is to bear "fruits worthy of repentance." John claimed that being the children of Abraham held no significant merit. Neither is claiming to be born again without the necessary fruit bearing.

John made clear that no matter what our pedigree, or how conscientious, "by-the-book" is our behavior, the wrath is sure, and God's judgment is imminent upon us who bear no fruit. Even now John claims the "axe is laid at the roots" (verse 10). In other words, the judgment process has already begun.

We must understand what this sign means. It's quite clear without the necessary fruit, the tree will be cut down from its roots. John is literally proclaiming there is not a safe place from God's wrath except for the necessary fruits of repentance.

If we are a true child of God, or a true minister of the Gospel, we will, like John, utter such words of warning. The people who are in our life are like our congregation. Are they not? As John, we must cry out to them, "Repent, you vipers."

At the beginning of this chapter, I mentioned how the Hale-Bopp comet revealed how believing false signs can be disastrous. The Heaven's Gate cult committed suicide. But God's soldiers must comprehend that believing false signs is committing suicide. Is not self-destruction, in fact, suicide?

If we're going to find our way to Heaven and overcome this life, we must learn the rules of the road and pay attention to the signs. They must be followed with care, lest we, by believing a false sign, take a wrong turn into disaster.

As always, I will build upon each chapter to have a firm foundation. This will reveal why many signs are not being heeded and some are being ignored, altogether, through false teaching.

Christian, hearken unto the signs. Pay attention to the rules of the road. These signs are not to discourage us, but to give the weaponry to endure and overcome. Heaven awaits those of us who are paying attention to the warning signs of the Scriptures and do not accept the false indicators of the time!

Chapter 2

Sign: Worthless Salt and Hidden Lights

> Ye are the salt of the earth: but if the salt have lost his savour, wherewith shall it be salted? It is thenceforth good for nothing, but to be cast out, and to be trodden under foot of men. Ye are the light of the world. A city that is set on a hill cannot be hid. Neither do men light a candle, and put it under a bushel, but on a candlestick; and it giveth light unto all that are in the house. Let your light so shine before men, that they may see your good works, and glorify your Father which is in heaven (Matthew 5:13–16).

IN THIS CHAPTER, WE'LL discuss worthless salt or salt that has lost its savour and hidden lights or lights that no longer shine.

WORTHLESS SALT

> Let your speech be always with grace, seasoned with salt, that ye may know how ye ought to answer every man (Colossians 4:6).

First of all, we'll discuss Matthew 5:13–16 and the importance of salt keeping its savor cannot be overemphasized. I know we think of salt as the seasoning on our table to enhance the flavor of our food.

But we need to understand if it has lost its taste, it's of no value to any of us. It's worthless salt.

We're supposed to be the salt of the earth to preserve the world from corruption and destruction. Yet, too many of God's soldiers have joined in the degeneracy of those around us. The necessity of separation is no longer being heeded. Many are joining in the so-called pleasures of this world to gratify the lust of the flesh, the lust of the eyes, and the pride of life.

The gravity in all this is that we've deceived ourselves into thinking we're still on the path to Heaven. However, the truth is all on the wide path leading to destruction are not going to inherit eternal life. When Christians make no effort to disturb the unrighteousness in the world, we have become worthless salt. We are not to be like the world, but to make them uneasy in their unholy life.

As salt stings a wound to bring forth healing, our life and our speech should sting their conscience in order for them to become uncomfortable in their unrighteousness. Prayerfully our salt will cause them to repent, and allow them to be healed.

Seasoning brings out the best in food. Our righteous life or being salt should bring out the best in those we have contact with. If our salt has lost its savor (its ability to make a difference), we'll continue to encourage the worst in people. This is a sad truth that we, by our lack of salt, have no effect upon their sinful life.

What we need to comprehend as salt seasons food, God's soldiers should improve and positively influence the people and society around us. If we understand salt is a preservative, it will enable us to fight immorality, degeneration, ungodliness, unrighteousness, etc. and preserve a godly influence in our society.

> I know thy works, that thou are neither cold nor hot: I would thou wert cold or hot. So then because thou art LUKEWARM, and neither cold nor hot, I will spue thee out of my mouth (Revelation 3:15–16).

If we lose our savor or the healing and preservative qualities of salt, we'll become spiritually "lukewarm." This condition suppresses or destroys the power and presence of the Holy Spirit in our lives. As a result, Christians who are no longer seasoned with salt will be "trodden under foot of men."

When we become lukewarm, we're apathetic and negligent about our devotion to Christ. We become lazy and lethargic in our service. We compromise with worldly standards and behaviors. Before long, we resemble and talk like the world and are no longer an illustration or example of Christ.

The Christians in the church at Laodicea claimed to be devoted to Christ, yet the Lord informed them of their spiritually wretched and miserable condition. He warned them of his judgment against the sin of being lukewarm. They were told to repent and turn from their own way and turn to God's way and accept forgiveness.

This is a frightening truth. If we are no longer salt stinging the ungodly lives of those around us, we will end up compromising and giving into the ways of the sinful society in which we live. To help clarify, see chapter four of my book, *Storms Are Faith's Workout*, where I explain about Lot and the results of his compromise. As we continue to do this, we walk more and more on the broad and wide path that will eventually lead to our destruction in the end.

Only through repentance can we be restored to a right relationship with the Lord. As we remain devoted, strong in our faith, and overcome the lukewarm Christianity that is predominate today, will we be granted the right to sit with him in his throne (Revelation 3:21).

Salt that doesn't lose its savor, but remains potent in its ability to season and preserve will continue to be a thorn in the flesh of those around us. At the same time, it will keep our life seasoned, preserved, and prevent us from becoming worthless salt.

HIDDEN LIGHTS

The light of the body is the eye: if therefore thine eye be single, thy whole body shall be full of light. But if thine eye be evil, thy whole body shall be full of darkness. If therefore the light that is in thee be darkness, how great is that darkness! (Matthew 6:22–23).

If the light of the body is the eye, how careful we must be to guard what we subject ourselves to. We need to think of our eye as being the lenses of a camera that imprint images into our minds. What impressions are we placing into our thoughts? Are we leaving images that will lead to holy, godly, and pure thoughts? Are they reflections that will leave behind corruption?

> If we say that we have fellowship with him, and walk in darkness, we lie, and do not the truth: but if we walk in the light, as he is in the light, we have fellowship one with another, and the blood of Jesus Christ his Son cleanseth us from all sin (1 John 1:6–7).

If our eye is single or good, we will walk in the light. If our eye is evil, we walk in darkness. When we walk in darkness, we live outside of God's truth and have no fellowship or companionship with him. Walking in darkness (an eye that is evil) rejects God's standards for our life and chooses to live according to the standards of the world or our carnal nature.

We decide to allow our eye to be single or good by what we allow into our lives, what we see, what we hear, what we read, what we entertain, etc. As we control what our eye comes in contact with, we walk in his light and have fellowship with Christ.

The simple question to ask ourselves is are we a beacon of light or a shroud of darkness to those we interact with. We are either one or the other. Today's compromising has many of God's soldiers hiding our light for fear of being ridiculed, mocked, etc.

However, let's consider the importance of being a light in this dark world. As God's soldiers, we are to provide light in the spiritual darkness around us. We should be as a lighthouse guiding the ships through the stormy sea to safety.

As a light, we are to be the means whereby God is enabled to enlighten the minds of those we bring the gospel message to. However, how many professing to be Christians have hid our light in the darkness by compromising truth, desiring to be part of the crowd, fear of rejection, or participating in sin?

Our lives should stand out of the darkness as the lighthouse on the hill. After all, genuine faith in Christ cannot be hid. Yet, how many can't be deciphered from the world? Where is our light? Why is our light not shining? Why is our life not exposing the darkness of sin?

The sun is lighted up in the firmament of the heavens to diffuse its light and heat freely to every inhabitant of the earth. The lamp is not hid under a bushel, but is placed where it may give light to all in the house. This is what every believer in Christ ought to be. Our light should spread the light of heavenly knowledge, the need to repent of sin, and the warmth of God's love to all we come in contact with.

As we preserve our salt and be a lighthouse on the hill, we will not only preserve ourselves and shed light on our life, but will sting the sin in the lives of those we have contact with.

False indicators are destructive as seen in the group that committed suicide through misinterpreting the Hale-Bopp comet. If we are to avoid believing false indicators, we must not become worthless salt or allow our light to be hidden!

Chapter 3

Sign: False Doctrines

> Jesus answered them, and said, My doctrine is not mine, but his that sent me. If any man will do his will, he shall know of the doctrine, whether it be of God, or whether I speak of myself (John 7:16–17).

> Then said Jesus to those Jews which believed on him, If ye continue in my word, then are ye my disciples indeed. And ye shall know the truth, and the truth shall make you free. (John 8:31–32).

I MUST ADMIT IGNORANCE in the church today has me somewhat bewildered. If we truly have eyes to see, we would see how grieved the Holy Spirit is at our lack of knowledge, our illiteracy of Scriptural truth.

Countless times, I have professing Christians inform me they don't want to get into doctrine. It's just simple faith in Jesus. We don't have to have a doctoral degree. Why study what's not necessary to salvation? There are too many differences of opinion in doctrine, and we don't want to get into that. It's just not important.

While it is simple faith in Christ, there is too much ignorance and lack of knowledge in believers. We need to know what God desires for our life. Without sound doctrine (guidelines, rules, principles), we become ignorant. In fact, we are as unenlightened as those who are not regenerated.

My people are destroyed for lack of knowledge (Hosea 4:6).

There are four concepts (principles) as to why doctrine is vital, essential, critical to our spiritual growth.

1. To know what we believe.
2. To know why we believe.
3. To believe what we know.
4. To act on what we know.

What is doctrine? If I asked God's soldiers that question. How many could answer me? I mean answer me so that I totally understand what doctrine is.

Let me give some definitions of doctrine.

1. That which is taught, instructed, educated, tutored.
2. Bible doctrine is "Bible truths arranged in a systematic and authoritative form."
3. It is a belief. WHAT WE BELIEVE.

Doctrine is my education, my instruction. It's what I have been taught. It's what I believe. Let's keep the statement that doctrine is what I believe in mind as we go on.

So, my doctrine is what I believe. It's my foundation upon which I build my faith walk. Now, is what I believe, the truth? But what is truth? How do I know truth? How do I find truth?

> Jesus saith unto him, I am the way, the truth, and the life:
> no man cometh to the Father but by me (John 14:6).

For truth, I must look to Jesus. It's only Jesus who will lead me to the Father and Heaven.

> In the beginning was the Word, and the Word was with
> God, and Word was God. The same was in the beginning
> with God. All things were made by him; and without
> him was not any thing made that was made. . . He was
> in the world, and the world was made by him, and the
> world knew him not. . . And the Word was made flesh,
> and dwelt among us, (and we beheld his glory, the glory

as of the only begotten of the Father,) full of grace and truth (John 1:1–14).

These Scriptures in John chapter 1 reveal that Jesus is the word of God made flesh. So, if we want to know truth, we must look to the word of God or Jesus. There's no other way to truth, except through God's word.

> So then faith cometh by hearing, and hearing by the word of God (Romans 10:17).

Now, if Jesus is the truth and He is the word, true doctrine is found only in him. Where do we find him? In the Bible, for He is the word of God. What must we do to acquire sound doctrine?

1. We must study doctrine, as surely as we need oxygen to breathe.
2. It is essential that we know what the word of God teaches.
3. We need to know why we believe what we believe.
4. No one in the world can give us Biblical faith.
5. As we are taught the word of God, we will be enabled to communicate what we believe.

The first Christian theologian to attempt any systematic exposition of the concept of truth was Augustine who declared, "The word of God, Jesus Christ, is the truth because He expresses the Father."

It's critical that we go to the word to find truth. Only in the word of God can we know the particulars of what we believe, and the reason for our belief. Only the wise man/woman of God bases, builds, and establishes belief on the word of God, and the word of God only.

> All scripture is given by inspiration of God, and is profitable for doctrine, for reproof, for correction, for instruction in righteousness: That the man of God may be perfect, throughly furnished unto all good works (2 Timothy 3:16–17).

Scripture or the word of God is the doctrine (teaching) that furnishes us with the knowledge needed to perfect or mature us in the faith.

We need to study Scripture to know whether what we hear is being interpreted in the light of the full counsel of Scripture, or if there is error in the teaching which could lead us astray. It's our responsibility to recognize false doctrine and not follow it.

> Study to shew thyself approved unto God, a workman that needeth not to be ashamed, rightly dividing the word of truth (2 Timothy 2:15).

If we don't base our doctrine, what we have been taught, or what the will of God is, from a knowledge gained from accurately interpreting the whole of Scripture, we will be led into false doctrines. We don't take a Scripture and base our doctrine or belief on it. Rightly dividing means that all doctrine is backed up in the whole of Scripture and not in pulling out a Scripture to form our foundation for what we want to believe.

The Bible writers were God's instruments in communicating his will to men (1 Peter 1:21). It is his "word" because He speaks to us in its sacred pages. Whatever the inspired writers declare in the Bible is true and binding upon us, because God declares it's Holy Spirit inspired and therefore all doctrine should line up with the whole of Scripture.

> And the brethren immediately sent away Paul and Silas by night unto Berea: who coming thither went into the synagogue of the Jews. These were more noble than those in Thessalonica, receiving the word with all readiness of mind, and searched the scriptures daily, whether those things were so (Acts 17:10–11).

What the Bereans did is what all Christians should do. We should never accept the interpretation of Scripture from a minister, teacher, family member, etc. as set in stone. Our revelations must be Holy Spirit interpretation of the whole of Scripture and not because we were taught it by man. When the Bereans "searched" the word, they examined or made careful and exact research. Whenever we hear a sermon or teaching, we, like the Bereans, should become Bible students to verify the validity of what we've heard.

Whatever the word of God teaches is therefore, the only truth that's accepted by God. Therefore, if what we believe is not backed up in the teaching (doctrine) of the whole word of God, it's wrongly divided or biased. That's why it's imperative to study the Bible ourselves to make sure what we're being taught is solid and not misleading.

In John 8:31-32, Jesus implies that many who profess themselves to be Christ's disciples are not. It's only as we continue in Christ's word that we shall be accepted as his disciples.

> Jesus answered them, Verily, verily, I say unto you, Whosoever committeth sin is the servant of sin. And the servant abideth not in the house for ever: but the Son abideth ever. If the Son therefore shall make you free, ye shall be free indeed (John 8:34-36).

How do we know if we are continuing in his word or in truth and that we are truly his disciple? Jesus makes clear in the above Scripture. He tells us we've been freed from the power of sin.

This reveals true doctrine is visible in our life. We're easily recognized, because we're no longer in bondage to sin. In order to remain free from the power of sin, we must abide (linger, stay, tarry) in the word of God.

We must constantly be aware of what the word says. How can we know sin (as God sees it), if we look elsewhere. We'll never know God's will by listening to false ministers, false doctrines, ear ticklers, etc. that please and pamper our flesh.

Preachers of itching ears will never show us the way to the Father. They'll entice us to walk on the wide and broad path that leads to destruction. It's the complete opposite of the straight and narrow that leads to the Father and eternal life.

We will never know truth or what God expects of our lives, unless we listen to his doctrine which is his teaching. The teaching of the word of God is the only true doctrine that leads to the Father.

As we abide in his word, we gain a greater knowledge of the truth. Only truth sets us free from sin. Our soul must be purified, before it can give up its own desires and indulgences. The word of God (the doctrine or teaching of God) is what stirs up our duty to God, and works a total change in our life.

God's soldiers must be watchful against all spiritual dangers and enemies. We must guard against erroneous, unholy, and false doctrine. These teachings are contrary to the truth of Scripture.

We must also be careful not to be so dogmatic in what we believe that we are unteachable. Too many times, Christians believe what we have been taught and pull out our pet verses to argue our point. Yet, other Scriptures will reveal our belief is not balanced by the whole of God's word. That's why the Scriptures are better interpreted by the Spirit that giveth life and not the letter that killeth.

All who claim to know Christ should walk according to the word of God. If we're not, according to Christ, we're not his disciples.

True doctrine exposes that Christians must walk in holiness and not in sin. A mere outward profession is nothing. It must be backed up by the evidence of a holy life and holy conduct.

Now, if doctrine is what we believe, then our belief is our doctrine. In other words, what we believe is the principles, rules, standards, laws, precepts, grounds, reasons, motives, instructions by which we live. We're instructed or taught by what we believe.

Let me give a little example of being taught wrongly and believing it's correct.

Several years ago, a mother told me that she and her young daughter were perusing an encyclopedia, when the child saw the words "Rhode Island," She was aghast to find the encyclopedia had misspelled "Road."

When her mother proceeded to tell her that the Rhode in Rhode Island is spelled "R-H-O-D-E."

The child claimed her teacher said she had spelled it correctly when she wrote Road Island on her paper. She was unyielding no matter what her mother said. In other words, she called her mother and the encyclopedia a LIAR.

What she believed was not based upon true doctrine (teaching). She had been incorrectly instructed and her belief was based upon false doctrine. Her belief system was founded upon a lie. Because of this false teaching, she was now trying to instruct, teach, or tutor her mother in the lie.

I know this is a simple example to comprehend. Sometimes, simplicity can help us learn a truth more easily. This illustration is to reveal we could be abiding in wrong doctrine, wrong teaching, wrong instruction, and be convinced it's truth. Too many Christians have become unteachable because we believe what was taught by our preacher, our parents, our denomination, etc. We refuse to allow the Holy Spirit to enlighten us to truth and have become dogmatic or inflexible in what we've been taught like the child in my illustration.

This is why doctrine is so vital. We must know that what we believe is truth built upon the truth of God's word and not Scripture pulled out to fit that belief or mixed with the traditions of men, fables, etc.

There are many deceivers claiming to be ministers of God who are deceiving and being deceived (2 Timothy 3:13). These will lead astray all who listen to them. Man is prone to be a lover of self. It's the desire to please self more than God which causes us to compromise God's word.

Self lovers merely have an outward profession, there's not real evidence of a holy life and conduct. Too many are professing Christ with mouth service, but in daily life (behavior), there's evidence of a sinful life.

What is being taught is another doctrine. It's not what Jesus or his word teaches. What I'm trying to say is that if doctrine is instruction, then our life (the way we live) instructs and teaches others.

> Ye are our epistle written in our hearts; known and read
> of all men (2 Corinthians 3:2).

This is serious stuff. Paul said all men are reading our lives. Our lives instruct and teach all those who come in contact with us. If our doctrine, instruction, teaching is not based on truth of Jesus Christ, it is false. In other words, if our life is a teacher, and our teaching or our life is not portraying Christ, we are a false teacher of false doctrine. If our life is representing Christ, it is based on Christ or truth, and we are a true teacher of sound doctrine.

Are we seeing the importance of the word of God being studied? We must read, read, read, study, study, study doctrine or the teachings of Christ. Only as we know the word of God, can we portray Christ, know what is truth, and perceive when we hear false doctrine. Our knowledge of God's word will shed light on the darkness of false teachers and false doctrine!

Chapter 4

Sign: False Ministers

Verily, verily, I say unto you, he that entereth not by the
door into the sheepfold, but climbeth up some other way,
the same is a thief and a robber. But he that entereth in by
the door is the shepherd of the sheep. To him the porter
openeth; and the sheep hear his voice: and he calleth his
own sheep by name, and leadeth them out. And when
he putteth forth his own sheep, he goeth before them,
and the sheep follow him: for they know his voice. And
a stranger will they not follow, but will flee from him: for
they know not the voice of strangers. This parable spake
Jesus unto them: but they understood not what things
they were which he spake to them. Then said Jesus unto
them again, verily, verily, I say unto you, I am the door of
the sheep. All that ever came before me are thieves and
robbers: but the sheep did not hear them. I am the door:
by me if any man enter in, he shall be saved, and shall go
in and out, and find pasture. The thief cometh not, but
for to steal, and to kill, and to destroy: I am come that
they might have life, and that they might have it more
abundantly (John 10:1–10).

A PREDOMINANT SIGN TODAY is the flocking of those professing
to be Christians to hear false teachers. These false ministers are
followed as if they are the *Pied Piper*.

When Jesus used this illustration or allegory, people of his
day knew what He was referring to. Of course today, we don't have

much understanding of shepherds and sheep except for what we may have heard.

But whether or not we are farmers, whether or not we comprehend shepherd and sheep is irrelevant. What's important is we understand what Jesus was teaching through this allegory.

The spiritual principle being illustrated must be understood. It's not imperative for us to know shepherds or sheep, because we do know about ministers and congregations. This is the crux of the allegory to be understood.

Yes, Jesus does claim to be the good shepherd, but a careful observation to the verses reveals Christ is disclosing much more than the fact of him being the good shepherd.

He was, in fact, teaching us how to recognize who and what false ministers are. It's imperative for the sheep (God's soldiers) who follow ministers to know if they are true or false ministers.

Christ wanted us to know and recognize any minister who does not enter into the sheepfold by the door (Jesus) but climbs up some other way are thieves and robbers. Jesus wants us to comprehend this. If someone claims to be a minister then he/she must enter the sheepfold by the door.

> And he gave some, apostles; and some, prophets; and some, evangelists; and some, pastors and teachers; For the perfecting of the saints, for the work of the ministry, for the edifying of the body of Christ (Ephesians 4:11–12).

Jesus Christ is the door who calls the ministers to be shepherds. Today, it seems so-called apostles, prophets, etc. are crawling out of the woodwork. It's a scary time we live in when scores claim to be an apostle, prophet, etc. Man is being self-called or man-called, and Jesus is not in it.

The Lord has made clear to my spirit how grieved He is at the amount of false ministers running rampant through the Body of Christ and leading believers astray by false doctrines, doctrines of devils, charismatic personality, etc.

Many are falling prey to these false ministers, because they don't comprehend the criteria. The first requirement to be a minister is a genuine call from Christ. It's not some man/woman going to someone and informing them of a call to ministry. It's not our thinking that we'd make a good minister, etc. If we are called, Jesus will tell us.

Let me explain something here. As we know we are born again, because we have an experience with the living God, we know we are called to the ministry. It's an experience we can't forget any more than we can forget our salvation experience.

It's not something we can forget because it's a definite occurrence. Hear me, this isn't taught in many churches. What I'm trying to convey in this chapter is that as salvation is an unforgettable experience, the baptism in the Holy Spirit is an unforgettable experience, and so is any call to ministry.

Just because we go to Bible College, have degrees, etc. doesn't establish a call to ministry. Too many are going off to Bible College or Seminary to be trained as ministers. This is sad that we can be trained or tutored how to preach, etc. However, if we don't enter by the door (a genuine call from Christ to ministry), we are a false minister who climbed in some other way.

All who climb over (those who call themselves or are called by man/woman) are not sanctioned by the Holy Spirit. He will not put his stamp of approval upon any self-called, man-called, man-trained, etc. minister. Yes, multitudes will follow their fleshly hype because man wants to have his flesh stirred. However, all such ministers are a thief and robber of the sheep and not a shepherd who loves and cares for them. They love the accolades, the money, the prosperous life, the lavish vacation, the pricey homes, etc. but many in their congregation live in abject poverty.

Don't get me wrong, I know the laborer is worthy of his hire. But he/she is not to live like a king/queen off the sacrifice of the congregation. There needs to be a balance in the lifestyle of the ministers and the congregation. Jesus had no place to lay his head. Paul was a tentmaker. Ministers are to be honored and respected but not worshipped and put on a pedestal.

Listen to me, if we claim to be a minister, we know the value of the souls under us. We comprehend Jesus Christ died and shed his blood for each soul. That's how valuable each sheep is to Jesus and any Christ-called minister comprehends the true riches of the men, women, and children God has entrusted in our care.

When God places us in ministry, we are caretakers of the souls Jesus died for. We're the watchmen of God's flock to make sure no evil, no foes get near our flock. A God called shepherd will be like David who protected his father's sheep. When the lion and the bear came at the lambs, he slew them both (1 Samuel 17:34–35).

I'm telling you when we have a call on our life, it will drive us to our knees weeping before God for those who are going wayward. Our heart will sense God's heart who desires that none should perish, but all should come to repentance (2 Peter 3:9).

It's the responsibility of God's ministers to study the word of God to properly feed his Father's sheep. Without a proper understanding of the word, we can't feed the necessary nutrients needed for spiritual health and growth.

Yes, it's the responsibility for a minister to be sure of his/her calling, give proper spiritual food to strengthen the spiritual condition of our Father's sheep. However, it's the responsibility of each and every believer to make sure they recognize the false ministers.

If we allow ourselves to be led astray by a false apostle, prophet, evangelist, pastor, or teacher, we will not be able to blame the minister come judgment day. It was our choice to allow them to take us down the wrong road. We chose to pamper our flesh and not to crucify or deny it. We are guilty of neglecting the study of God's word that will lead us into all truth, give knowledge and wisdom of the things of God, and help us discern good and evil.

> Study to shew thyself approved unto God, a workman that needeth not to be ashamed, rightly dividing the word of truth (2 Timothy 2:15).

We are commanded to know God's word, in order to rightly divide its truth. If we have a knowledge of the Scriptures, and we hear something that doesn't bear witness with our spirit as being truth, it's our responsibility to stop listening to the minister or anyone who teaches whatever is contrary to sound doctrine.

In my book, *God: The Holy Spirit: The Conquering Power Within*, I told of a story about when I was first saved. There were several going around with so-called personal prophecies after a Bible study. It did not bear witness with my spirit, and the Holy Spirit told me to leave and not go back. After a while, I heard the Pastor of the church, I attended, had shut it down. He said they were giving place to seducing spirits.

It's not an easy task to tell believers the truth today, for many are looking for the ministers who will tickle their ears. Hearing the truth will constrict our flesh and make it uneasy. But without the discomfort on our flesh, we'll never learn to deny self and overcome this life.

I've had some I know who are living in sins that will not inherit the kingdom of God going around telling others about their great vision from God, the great revelation God gave them, etc. They speak with such cunning and are listened to by those who should know God's word.

Hear me, foolish believers are listening to them as if they are an oracle of God. Furthermore, many are claiming to be ministers and have congregations being led to Hell through false doctrines. They compromise the word of God to the allurement of those who don't want to deny their flesh what it desires.

A corrupt tree cannot bring forth good fruit. God did not give the adulterer, fornicator, hireling, etc. claiming to be God's minister, any vision or revelation. God's soldiers must wake up to this truth. God does not bless a sinful life, and He is not giving them any vision or revelation. They may have received something, but it was NOT of God. The Holy Spirit will never encourage a sinful life.

We live in a time where believers want one foot in Christ and the other foot in the pleasures of this world. It doesn't work that way. As stated earlier, we are either hot or cold. We have to be for Christ, or we are for the world.

All false ministers are sent by Satan and not Jesus. They are thieves and robbers, who will preach and teach a compromising, flesh appealing, false message, while prospering at the expense of those under them. Listen to me, they may use the word, as the devil did when tempting Christ, but it will never be rightly divided. It will be given in a manner to lead astray from truth. Because God didn't place them as shepherds of his sheep, those who follow them will be destroyed.

True ministers of God are sent forth with a message of repentance and deliverance. This message is how we discern those who are God's shepherds. A perfect example is John the Baptist who came forth preaching a message of repentance and deliverance.

We'll know the genuine called of God ministers by their fruit. There will be a holiness about them. There will be a meekness about them even though there's going to be a boldness because they will walk in the authority God has given.

We can't change that authority whether we are male or female. The authority in the ministry is still there. One of the main attributes about God-called ministers is the ability to unfold the word of God. Such ministers are enabled to open the word and feed the sheep. Christ gives pastors (ministers) according to his heart who will feed knowledge and understanding (Jeremiah 3:15).

It's imperative for God's soldiers to become fruit inspectors of those claiming to be ministers of the Lord. In other words, we must try the spirit of who we listen to and discern if the teaching or preaching is spirit enlightening to encourage holy living or flesh appealing to encourage sinful living.

Let me explain a little further about false ministers. In Kings chapter 22, King Jehoshaphat asked if there were any other prophets. The King of Israel said there was one, but he never prophesies good but evil concerning me. Whereas, the other four-hundred all prophesied good toward him. Therefore, he enjoyed hearing from the false prophets, because they tickled his ears and appealed to his flesh.

Another example is Elijah who stood against four-hundred-fifty false prophets. Also, during the time just before Judah fell, Jeremiah was the only prophet still warning Judah. Because of his steadfastness to truth, he was put in the dungeon by the King of Judah. He warned if they did not surrender, they would be killed.

All the false prophets prophesy "Peace, Peace, we are coming into a time of peace. We are going to have perfect peace." Whereas, Jeremiah was warning there would be no peace.

What this chapter is meant to teach is that as it was 400 to 1 in Jehoshaphat's day and 450 to 1 in Elijah's day, so it is today. There are a multitude of false ministers/prophets/pastors proclaiming an ear tickling message and multitudes are blindly following them down the broad and wide road. In order to overcome and inherit eternal life, we must quit following false ministers who tickle our flesh and seek out ministers who will make our flesh uncomfortable!

Chapter 5

Sign: Lethargic Zeal

Not slothful in business; fervent in spirit; serving the Lord (Romans 12:11).

And now, little children, abide in him; that, when he shall appear, we may have confidence, and not be ashamed before him at his coming. If ye know that he is righteous, ye know that every one that doeth righteousness is born of him (1 John 2:28–29).

Being born again, not of corruptible seed, but of incorruptible, by the word of God, which liveth and abideth for ever (1 Peter 1:23).

THE LORD HAS REVEALED there is a lifeless zeal for righteousness in many claiming to be Christians. A great many of us have become complacent and sit in the pew of do-nothing. We go to church and sit there in a state of fake righteousness, when, in fact, our lives outside of church reflect unrighteousness.

It's not what we pretend to be in church, but what we exhibit at home, work, etc. that reveals who we really are. What do we talk about? How do we treat others? What do we meditate upon? What do we listen to? What do we watch or read? Are we meditating on God's word or the words of false ministers? Are we listening to those teaching an ear tickling message? Are we watching, reading, and believing what these false ministers say?

It's a sad truth, but many are deceiving themselves. We can't take in corruption and not have corruption come out. If we believe we can sow something and not reap what has been sown, we are deceived (Galatians 6:9). If we believe evil communications will not corrupt our life, we are deceived (1 Corinthians 15:33).

Are we showing forth the praises of him who called us out of darkness and translated us in to his marvelous light? (1 Peter 2:9). How many times do we leave church and go forth to gossip, indulge in sin, and grieve the Holy Spirit?

It's a distressing truth, but many of God's soldiers are alienating themselves from God because of hypocritical lives. We no longer have a godly zeal, but a lethargic zeal that has become dull and lifeless.

Because of this, we just sit by and allow ourselves to be influenced by the ungodliness and unrighteousness around us. It's like Lot who moved his tent too close to Sodom and when he tried to warn others of the coming destruction, he was ridiculed by those who were to be his sons-in-law (Genesis 19:14).

If we're not doing whatever pleases God, we are, in fact, taking in corruption. We are not to fellowship with what is contrary to God's word. Yet, how many are heaping to themselves false ministers? Instead of being zealous for righteousness, most are seeking to hear that sinful indulgence is accepted by God. After all, a God of love will never send us to Hell.

> So that we ourselves glory in you in the churches of God for your patience and faith in all your persecutions and tribulations that ye endure: Which is a manifest token of the righteous judgment of God, that ye may be counted worthy of the kingdom of God, for which ye also suffer: Seeing it is a righteous thing with God to recompense tribulation to them that trouble you; And to you who are troubled rest with us, when the Lord Jesus shall be revealed from heaven with his mighty angels, In flaming fire taking vengeance on them that know not God, and that obey not the gospel of our Lord Jesus Christ: Who shall be punished with everlasting destruction from the presence of the Lord, and from the glory of his power, When he shall come to be glorified in his saints, and to

> be admired in all them that believe (because our testimony among you was believed) in that day. Wherefore also we pray always for you, that our God would count you worthy of this calling, and fulfil all the good pleasure of his goodness, and the work of faith with power. That the name of our Lord Jesus Christ may be glorified in you, and ye in him, according to the grace of our God and the Lord Jesus Christ (2 Thessalonians 1:4–12).

Scripture is clear that Christ is coming back, and He will severely punish sin. The lackadaisical zeal for righteousness in those claiming to be Christians will find themselves being the recipients of his flaming fire that is the recompense of all who lived in unrighteousness.

> He that saith, I know him, and keepeth not his commandments, is a liar, and the truth is not in him (1 John 2:4).

We can't claim to know Christ and live in sin. Our keeping his word reveals the truth is in us and that we do know him. When Paul states Christ is coming back in flaming fire to take vengeance on those who obey not the gospel, he is also talking about lukewarm Christians who are not keeping the word of God. Christ makes clear they will be vomited out of his mouth if there is no repentance (Revelation 3:16).

Christ is coming back for a righteous people, not a people who have indulged in unrighteous living. We can't expect to be rewarded for our lack of holiness, lack of godliness, and lack of righteousness. We sit and watch ungodly television shows, movies, etc. Some indulge in pornography, fornication, adultery, homosexuality, lies, and other corruption. Whereas, if we would keep allowing the incorruptible seed of God's word to grow in us, we would be zealous for righteousness.

If we take one bad apple and put it in a bushel of apples, will that bushel of apples turn the bad apple into a good one? Of course not. The bad apple is going to corrupt all those around. It will spread until the whole bushel is corrupted. We can't take in a little corruption and expect to remain uncontaminated.

How many times have we seen Christians with a zeal at first. There's a genuine fervor for Christ, but we won't let go of that little leaven. Before long, the corruption spreads and spreads until corruption has caused us to lose our zeal and eventually stop living a righteous life.

It's essential for God's soldiers to have a zeal for righteousness, for we need to be consecrated to him. Christians need to be separated from this world. If we have a zeal for righteousness, godliness, and holiness, we will shun the so-called pleasures of this world and its corruption of the soul.

When Jesus walked this earth, He was the self-revelation of God the Father. We, as the children of God, should be a self-revelation of Jesus in and through our lives. God's soldiers are extremely lacking a zeal. Therefore, most are a self-revelation of the flesh.

That's a hard saying, but only truth will set us free from our lethargic zeal. Our Scripture text in 1 John 2:29 is quite clear that only as we do righteousness are we born of him.

1 Corinthians 15:33–34 warns us about being deceived into thinking evil communications will not corrupt us. Many who are actually born of God have lost their zeal, have become lukewarm, are in a serious state of deception, and are about to go shipwreck. For more understanding about spiritual shipwreck, I recommend my book: *Spiritual Shipwreck on the Horizon: Exhorting Christians to Contend for the Faith and Comprehend the Deceitfulness of Sin.*

There are so few living a righteous life. Sitting in the pews with the lukewarm Christians, listening to their evil communications, and fellowshipping with them, has corrupted what was a separated life. Remember a little leaven will leaven or corrupt the whole.

If God's soldiers were hearing about the dangers of lukewarm Christianity's evil communications from the pulpit, there would be an awareness to avoid it. The truth is not preached from many pulpits, and it definitely isn't being taught out of the pulpit by lukewarm Christianity.

The disturbing truth is most in the church can't discern that lukewarm Christianity is of the same spirit as the world. Christian, awake out of slumber and realize the anti-Christ spirit is running rampant in many churches and in many claiming to be ministers.

We are either for Christ or we are against him. Being eighty, ninety, or even ninety-nine percent for Christ will give place to the anti-Christ spirit. If we are not one-hundred percent for Jesus, we give place to the devil to deceive.

There's so much false teaching from the pulpits that we who possess a righteousness zeal could begin to think something's wrong with us. We could start to think we're not doing what's right. However, that's the spirit of anti-Christ with its evil communications trying to deceive our thinking and weaken our resolve.

We can't allow such negativity to be planted in our mind. Only as we overcome, will we inherit all things. Because the gap between the world and lukewarm Christianity is closing up, we can't permit any evil communication to distract us from our goal.

> For if we sin willfully after that we have received the knowledge of the truth, there remaineth no more sacrifice for sins, But a certain fearful looking for of judgment and fiery indignation, which shall devour the adversaries. He that despised Moses' law died without mercy under two or three witnesses: Of how much sorer punishment, suppose ye, shall he be thought worthy, who hath trodden under foot the Son of God, and hath counted the blood of the covenant, wherewith he was sanctified, an unholy thing, and hath done despite unto the Spirit of grace? (Hebrews 10:26–29).

If God's soldiers continue to be seduced and seduced by the false ministers, the evil communications around, the corruption of the world, there will be no overcoming. It will be apostasy that awaits God's judgment. If we do despite the Spirit of grace, we willfully rebel against the Holy Spirit. Ignoring the conviction of the Spirit will lead to the death of a zeal for righteousness.

One of the problems for this decline in zeal is the church today is a replica of the Corinthian Church. We are born-again, baptized in the Holy Spirit, flowing in the gifts, but living like the devil.

Christian, awake to righteousness. Get out of the bed of lethargy. Get out of the seat of complacency. We are sleeping while souls are on a greased-pole to Hell. Furthermore, much of the church is dying and don't even know it.

The consuming fire, the refiners fire isn't burning in most anymore. The fact the zeal for righteousness has died exposes the absence of the Holy Spirit and fire cleansing process. When the zeal is consuming, it will condemn all unrighteousness in our life. It will give the desire to separate from the world. We'll want to be severed from all that is unholy and ungodly.

How many claiming to be Christians are going around with water pots to quench the zeal in us who are allowing the cleansing fire to burn? Our zeal makes them look bad. I know this to be true. When I was a young Christian, it was constantly done to me. Once I recognized the water pots, it was as if their water seemed to inflame my zeal.

God wants us to have a zeal for righteousness. We need a knowledge of the word (the incorruptible seed) that will enable us to go forth wise as serpents and as harmless as doves. We will seem like innocent doves while making surges in the ocean of Satan's power.

Too many are allowing the devil's ocean to remain calm and smooth. However, we who have a righteous zeal are going to get in there and start rocking those boats and shake up that ocean of unrighteousness, ocean of ungodliness, ocean of evil.

Because lukewarm Christianity is becoming so great, those who have an active and living zeal for righteousness will recognize the wheat and tares in the church. As we disrupt their calm sea, we'll be persecuted, ridiculed, mocked, called haters, bigots, etc.

Christ is coming back, and He will destroy all who do not obey his word. The church is deceiving itself into thinking that Jesus will not destroy believers who said the sinner's prayer. Because we have neglected to awake to righteous living, have become hearers only and not doers of the word, and are committing the sins that will not inherit the kingdom of God, we will be the recipients of the flaming fire and fiery indignation of the Lord's judgment.

Too many claim a God of love, yet forget the God of justice who will take vengeance on those that do not know God and obey not the gospel of Christ. We are liars if we claim to know him and do not keep his commandments (1 John 2:4). God doesn't condone sin. He is a righteous and holy God. The church of compromise or lukewarm Christianity is not portraying a righteous God. Lethargic zeal has quenched the knowledge of God in our lives and in the lives we associate with.

Listen to me, lukewarm Christianity will be toppled over by their own sin. Sin in lives will consume and destroy. Once we recognize this truth, it will cause us to separate ourselves from lukewarm teachings, compromising teachings, sinful practices, and make a difference. As the early church stood against sin at the peril of their life, when is today's church going to stand up for Christ no matter what?

Let's rise up, fan the flames of our zeal for righteousness through the incorruptible word of God, and be the salt and light that is so desperately needed in these last days.

As the zeal for righteousness is burning in us, it's going to come out in our speech, actions, and every aspect of our lives. Because righteousness is opposite of unrighteousness, it will burn inside us with a zeal that consumes all ungodliness before it can become corruption in our life.

It will also make the church of compromise and lethargic zeal uncomfortable when we walk by. Because we are vessels of honor made of pure gold and silver, lukewarm Christianity will squirm and not even know why. Righteous zeal is not lethargic, it is vibrant and exposes all unrighteousness!

Chapter 6

Sign: Empty Houses

> Then will I sprinkle clean water upon you, and ye shall
> be clean: from all your filthiness, and from all your idols,
> will I cleanse you. A new heart also will I give you, and a
> new spirit will I put within you: and I will take away the
> stony heart out of your flesh, and I will give you an heart
> of flesh (Ezekiel 36:25–26).

ACCORDING TO EZEKIEL, BEFORE a new heart is put in, something
significant takes place. There seems to be a preparation. I call it a
pre-op procedure. Before the surgery can occur, there has to be a
cleansing, a whitening, a purifying, a disinfecting, etc.

Let's think of that in the natural. If we look in the surgical
room, we see those involved in the surgery all in clean clothing.
There is a thorough cleansing or scrubbing of hands. Of course, all
things are sterilized or purified before the surgery begins.

According to Ezekiel, before the surgery or surgical procedure
of a new heart takes place, God sprinkles clean water upon us, and
we shall be clean from all our filthiness and idols. God says He will
cleanse us, before He proceeds with the heart transplant.

Once the pre-op is done, God proceeds to implant the new
heart. A new heart, a heart of flesh, a heart given by God himself.

This new heart is to change the whole of our infected nature,
our corrupted or fallen nature, and give us new appetites, new desires, new passions, etc. In other words, the new heart from God is

given to purify and refine our appetites and passions which are the result of sin.

Let me be more clear to help us understand. What we need to comprehend is the heart is generally understood to mean all the affections and passions. With the new heart, the purified and refined heart, comes a new spirit.

> And be not conformed to this world: but be ye transformed by the renewing of your mind, that ye may prove what is that good, and acceptable, and perfect, will of God (Romans 12:2).

The new spirit is the renewing of our mind which enlightens our understanding, corrects our judgment, and refines our will.

Understand this. The first thing God does is the pre-op of cleansing, purifying, and whitening. We can't have a new heart without the necessary cleansing. Once we are saved, He does the heart transplant. The new heart is to replace our fallen nature with its old desires and lusts. Once the new heart is transplanted, He gives us a new spirit which renews our mind.

Before the transplant, our heart is stony, it is hard, impenetrable, and cold. Its passions and affections are unyielding and frozen. They are unaffected by heavenly things and give no credit or glory to God.

We are not able to give glory to God until He gives us the new heart. Our fallen nature with its passions and appetites are only concerned for the glory of self. We may mention God, but our stony heart is incapable of giving God his due glory.

> When the unclean spirit is gone out of a man, he walketh through dry places, seeking rest: and findeth none. Then he saith, I will return unto my house whence I came out; and when he is come, he findeth it empty, swept, and garnished. Then goeth he, and taketh with himself seven other spirits more wicked than himself, and they enter in and dwell there: and the last state of that man is worse than the first. Even so shall it be also unto this wicked generation (Matthew 12:43–45).

Now, let's look at Matthew's Gospel. These Scriptures are incredible. I mean what Matthew is revealing to us is remarkable.

For the longest time, I just looked at it as an unclean spirit. But after prayerful contemplation, I believe the Lord revealed it could also be the fallen nature, our old nature. Before casting judgment, let me unfold what I believe the Lord has shown. After all, not all who have pre-op and a new heart transplant have been possessed by unclean spirits. However, we are all possessed with the old sinful nature.

Let's keep unfolding. Think about what Matthew is revealing. A fallen corrupt spirit can have no rest, but in the human heart that welcomes pollution and corruption.

The soul of the person from whom he had been expelled by the power of Christ was to be kept out by prayer, faith, and watchfulness. The unclean spirit comes back because he has no rest since it was kicked out.

Now, he findeth the house empty, swept, and garnished. This is mind boggling. He finds it empty. Empty of what? The former inhabitant, not himself, but the one who kicked him out is no longer there.

So, the one who gave the transplant no longer resides there. This empty place is ready to receive another occupant. This denotes a soul that has lost the life and power of godliness, and the testimony of the Holy Spirit.

Listen up. How can this house or person become seven times worse than before? It's simple. With the light from the Holy Spirit, God came in and cleaned it up. He threw all the garbage along with the occupant (our old nature) out.

This is like remodeling a house. It's no longer what it was. It's a new creation. Now, instead of filling the house with God and his word, the house no longer busied its affections and desires with the things of God or hearkening to his word.

The house found denying itself of what it wanted too difficult. It gradually started to empty itself of love, meekness, or all the fruit of the Spirit. It stopped praying, reading the Bible, and ignored the quickening of the Holy Spirit. Now it was vacant or empty for the folly and fashion of this world to move in.

In other words, we now welcome our old nature with the lust of the flesh, the lust of the eyes, and the pride of life. We allow ourselves to become lukewarm to the things of God until righteousness is no longer our way of life. We start to yield to our flesh and suppress the quickening of the Holy Spirit. When that happens, our new heart or heart of flesh becomes hard, cold, and impenetrable by the conviction of the Holy Spirit until we completely live in our old nature.

> For if, after they have escaped the pollutions of the world through the knowledge of the Lord and Savior Jesus Christ, they are again entangled therein and overcome, the latter end is worse with them than the beginning. For it had been better for them not to have known the way of righteousness, than, after they have known it, to turn from the holy commandment delivered unto them (2 Peter 2:20–21).

However, what we must comprehend is that we can never go back to what we were before we were born again. Our latter end is worse than the beginning. Because the house was completely renovated and made new, we become seven times worse. That's what Matthew was conveying when he said the unclean spirit goes and gets seven others worse than himself.

> These are spots in your feasts of charity, when they feast with you, feeding themselves without fear: clouds they are without water, carried about of winds; trees whose fruit withereth, without fruit, twice dead, plucked up by the roots; Raging waves of the sea, foaming out their own shame; wandering stars, to whom is reserved the blackness of darkness forever (Jude 12–13).

Jude makes obvious this was a house that had received pre-op and the transplant of a new heart. How do I know this? Because the Scriptures reveal the house had fruit which withered until it had no fruit. It was a fruit bearer and allowed its fruit to wither until it no longer was bearing any fruit. It was now twice dead. How was it twice dead? It was a dead tree that had come alive through faith, it was a living tree bearing fruit, but then it withered and died again.

I am the true vine, and my Father is the husbandman. Every branch in me that beareth not fruit he taketh away: and every branch that beareth fruit, he purgeth it, that it may bring forth more fruit. Now ye are clean through the word which I have spoken unto you. Abide in me, and I in you. As the branch cannot bear fruit of itself, except it abide in the vine; no more can ye, except ye abide in me. I am the vine, ye are the branches: He that abideth in me, and I in him, the same bringeth forth much fruit: for without me ye can do nothing. If a man abide not in me, he is cast forth as a branch, and is withered; and men gather them, and cast them into the fire, and they are burned (John 15:1–6).

Now, according to Jude the fruit withered until it bore no fruit. It had died and was plucked up because the roots were lifeless. In other words, there was no longer any spiritual life in that tree. It had been spiritually alive, but turned from righteousness to unrighteousness until its fruit withered, no longer bore fruit, died, and was plucked up by the roots. It apostatized and became an empty house, void of the Holy Spirit.

John makes apparent that it happened because the branch refused to abide in Christ. God's soldiers must wake up to truth. We can't think if we live in our old nature, allow our fruit to wither and die, and no longer have life in our roots, after we have become born again that we will not become twice dead. Yes, Jesus will never leave us nor forsake us, but we can forsake and reject him by trodden him under foot, counting his blood that sanctified us an unholy thing, and do despite unto the Spirit of grace (Hebrews 10:29).

As Christians, we must constantly fill our house with prayer, the word of God, and bear the fruit of the Spirit. Only as we do that will we give no place for our old nature to re-inhabit or take control of our house. We must constantly deny self (our old nature) any footing with its corruption and wicked desires and continuously yield to the new nature to bear fruit. As we keep our house full of the Holy Spirit, God's word, stay in the vine, and bear fruit, it will never become an empty house!

Chapter 7

Sign: Unrighteousness

> Be not deceived: evil communications corrupt good manners. Awake to righteousness, and sin not; for some have not the knowledge of God: I speak this to your shame (1 Corinthians 15:33–34).

THIS CHAPTER IS MEANT to encourage an awareness of signs. A lack of righteousness working in our lives is the cause of many being void of the knowledge of God. The comprehension of God is only as illuminated as the degree of righteousness at work in us. Without righteousness, unrighteousness will control all we do. The degree of righteousness is contingent upon our learning to deny self.

Righteousness is defined as being upright, virtuous, or obedient to the divine or the moral law, as, "a righteous man hateth lying" (Proverbs 13:5). It is further understood or characterized by uprightness or morality, as "Lord God Almighty, true and righteous are thy judgments" (Revelation 16:7). Simply put, righteousness hates unrighteousness, immorality, wickedness, etc. and loves righteousness, morality, virtue, etc.

What does it mean to have a knowledge of God? The Greek word for knowledge in the above Scripture means, the fact or state of knowing; perception of fact or truth; clear and certain mental apprehension; acquaintance with facts, truth or principles from study or investigation.

The appeal to "awake to righteousness" is not a mild one, for it refers to waking up out of a drunken stupor. The degree of sleep is like an unconscious drunk in a state of oblivion. This is a harsh statement, nevertheless, it must be understood. We must awaken out of our senseless state of whatever will be will be. Instead of responding as God's soldiers, we sit idly by and let the devil gain ground that doesn't belong to him.

Because of the lack of righteousness in professing Christians, those around us do not have a clear understanding of who and what God is. It seems like many in the church are either ignorant of the standard of righteousness and holiness the Lord desires in us, or are just compromising sin to continue in it or to be accepted by people.

If we don't start living righteous lives and rebuke sin, the world will never know God. Let's face it, how many are claiming to be Christians and yet are living in known sins that will not inherit the kingdom of God. The world sees this and believes if he/she is going to heaven, so am I. There doesn't seem to be much difference in the professing Christian and the lost.

However lip service will never make the heart devoted to Christ. Why aren't many, who claim to be Christians, shamed by a lack of righteousness? It's because we are deceived into thinking that God loves us, and He understands our physical weaknesses. Yes, He does love us, and He understands our flesh. That's why Christ came here, lived a sinless life, and died the cruel death on the cross. It was to deliver us from the power of sin and enable us to live in righteousness and not unrighteousness. We are to be holy as He is holy (1 Peter 1:16).

God's soldier must not be deceived, for we are what we feed upon. If we feed on evil communications, we will be corrupted. We must be aware of the company we keep. We must not hang around (fellowship) with the world or any claiming to be Christians who do not live a righteous and holy life.

If we put a little leaven in the loaf, the whole will eventually be leavened or corrupted. Because the human nature lusts after evil or what is pleasing to the flesh, sin's leaven enters mankind and spreads quickly, while God's leaven of a new life spreads slowly. The old nature has an affinity towards evil and not God. For this reason, it's imperative for God's soldiers to avoid evil communications or the corruption around us.

We must wake up to what is right in politics, commerce, religion, and every facet of life. Before we can know what is right in these areas, we need to be aware of what is right in the eyes of God. In order to know what He considers right or wrong, we must have a knowledge of his word. The Bible reveals the mind of God or his view of things.

If the knowledge of God's word is to be attained, a study of his word has to be top priority. We have no grounds on which to claim ignorance, for the word of God is vastly available, especially to us who live in America. Thus, to have a lack of knowledge of what is right according to God is to be intentionally ignorant.

Politics has been an area much neglected by God's soldiers. We're not calling sin as sin as God's word clearly states. The Holy Spirit is grieved by our lack of standing against the evil taking over our country. We now have Muslims in government positions who refused to be sworn in on the Bible, the foundation for this "One Nation Under God."

The world says that the fetus or unborn child is not a human being. God's word says, "Before I formed thee in the belly I knew thee; and before thou camest forth out of the womb I sanctified thee, and I ordained thee a prophet unto the nations (Jeremiah 1:5). However, the politician not in favor of abortion is not a popular candidate for office.

Our court system has legalized the Sodom and Gomorrah lifestyle of the homosexuals, when God's word makes clear it is an abomination. To add to that, The Catholic Church has released a new book that reduces the "sin of Sodom" (Genesis 19:1–29) to "a lack of hospitality." Yet, the Genesis account clearly recounts the destruction of those cities because of the abhorrence to God. Let me explain. In Genesis 19:5, when the men wanted to "know" the two angels, it is the same word when Adam "knew" his wife.

In other words, the men wanted to have sex with them. Furthermore, Jude 8 claims that because Sodom and Gomorrah and the surrounding towns gave themselves up to sexual immorality and perversion (homosexuality), they serve as an example of those who will suffer the punishment of eternal fire.

The world is so bold with the blatant sins in commerce. Pornography is exhibited on newsstands and in department stores, while cable television brings obscenities into homes without a wink from most Christians. It's propagated on social media, etc. What has happened to God's soldiers? Do we not recognize evil, or are we pretending to be blind, deaf, and dumb for fear of ridicule?

Religion and false teaching is the biggest farce in the world today. It pretends to be godly, but it denies the power thereof. Even those claiming to be Christians are propagating good works as the way to God, whereas, the word plainly teaches Christ is the only way to God the Father (John 14:6).

False religion and false teachers have the loud voice in the world, and many are believing the lies proceeding forth from its mouth. The world doesn't know about false apostles, deceitful workers, transforming themselves into the apostles of Christ (2 Corinthians 11:13). However, God's soldiers know the final outcome of the worker of iniquity, and yet there seems to be little to no cry of warning. Where are the watchmen on the walls of America? Why are they holding their peace day and night?

The distressing truth is the lack of warning has come about because of sin in the church. Sin has climbed because we continuously compare ourselves with others to our downfall (2 Corinthians 10:12). What we have done is scale our standards against the world and think we are fine. The world has lowered themselves below the gutter and many in the church are just above the world (in the gutter). Christ is no longer God in our lives, and many are led by the flesh with all its lust of the flesh, the lust of the eyes, and the pride of life. Self has become god in our life. If we would do a fruit inspection, we might repent.

Instead of allowing the Holy Spirit to convict, we compare ourselves with someone who we believe is worse. When we do that, we're living farther and farther away from the righteousness Christ died to give us. As Christians, we are to compare ourselves to Jesus Christ. Once our hearts comprehend how great sin is to God, we'll stop giving excuses for our words, our lives, or our actions. We'll finally comprehend who and what we really are, and we'll no longer live in the gutter just a step above the standards of the world.

I know this chapter is somewhat intense, but too many cry about a lack of living in the conquering or overcoming power of the Holy Spirit. How can we expect to live in such power when we either indulge in sin or stand by and watch others falling into Hell because we give no warning out of fear of rejection from them?

We must view every facet of life in the light of God's word. This is the decision that differentiates us from the world. God's soldiers must constantly dwell on God's word, believe Jesus is coming back for those who have overcome sin in this life, believe we'll be resurrected from the dead, and believe Heaven or Hell awaits the resurrected. Only meditating upon these truths will cleanse us from sin, for we'll genuinely strive to overcome all sin in our life. This is contingent upon what we choose. Either we choose to deny self and strive to enter in at the straight gate, or we choose to indulge our flesh and enter in at the wide gate. The narrow way will lead to Heaven and only a few will find it. Broad is the way that leads to Hell and many will enter in thereat (Matthew 7:13–14).

The world is actively broadcasting sin, while God's soldiers are on the sidelines remaining quiet. Many sit in the seat of complacency and watch as the devil controls this country built upon the Judeo-Christian belief system. This is supposed to be a Christian Nation. God's soldiers must awaken out of slumber, lethargy, concession, compromise, etc. and stand on the side of God for righteousness.

A line has been drawn in the sand, and it's time to decide which side we're on. If we're for Christ, then stand against the unrighteousness prevailing in the church. Name sin as sin, come out of the world, put on the whole armor of God, tear down the strongholds trying to destroy this country, be a light and salt, and shake up the gates of Hell.

As we think about this, we understand evil communications will corrupt good manners. How true is it today as we look around and see the lack of righteousness not only in the world, but in the church. False teachers are proclaiming unsound doctrine and many so-called Christians are living in sin condoned by those who should be warning of its consequences.

Worldliness, unsound doctrine, false teachers, etc. are keeping those who Christ died to set free, chained in bondage to sin. God's soldiers continue to be deceived by evil communications. Lukewarm Christianity refuses to study the Bible that will reveal sin and its consequences, believes the interpretation of man instead of the Holy Spirit, and chooses to listen to the tickling ear preachers that pamper the flesh.

What happened to the zeal of the early church believers who willingly suffered ridicule, scourging, and martyrdom? If we believe Christ is returning for the overcomers, and the punishment of the wicked is Hell, where is our voice crying out against sin?

> He that overcometh shall inherit all things; and I will be
> his God, and he shall be my son (Revelation 21:7).

This should be a continual source of cleansing for God's soldiers. If we believe Heaven is worth fighting for, and Hell must be fought against, we should have the loudest voices warning the multitude to flee from the wrath to come.

Only those who overcome will inherit all things. The overcoming is this life and our inclination to sin when we are faced with temptations, storms, obstacles, tribulation, etc. As Christ overcame the power of sin, He has given us the same power through the indwelling Holy Spirit. We cannot believe we can live in unbelief or any kind of sin that will not inherit the kingdom of God and find ourselves in Heaven.

We cannot be deceived unless we have intentionally refused truth. Only the truth will set us free from sin, false doctrines, false teachers, etc. However, it will not go easy on our flesh, and that's the reason so many choose deception over truth.

God's soldiers must be hungry for the word of God, pray without ceasing, and walk in harmony with him daily. If these things are not done, we open ourselves up to false doctrines, teachers of itching ears, etc. A compromising gospel and false doctrines breed lukewarm Christianity that no longer contends for the faith.

It's imperative to watch the company we keep, the things we listen to, the things we see, the things we think, and the things we do. We must reflect, mirror, exhibit a righteous God who hates sin and punishes the wicked.

In order to be his representative in this world, we must portray a holy and just God in our lives. If we do not awaken to this reality, we'll not reveal a righteous God, and the world will not obtain the knowledge of God. Consequently, the message of God's coming judgment upon the wicked or worker of unrighteousness will not be hearkened, and we will be the leader of many following us to Hell.

This chapter was meant to be a wakeup call for God's soldiers to change the course of their lukewarm Christianity into fire breathing soldiers. The righteousness which God requires has not changed. Those claiming to be Christians and filled with the Holy Spirit have made him appear to lack power, because we continue in sin. As He enabled Christ to conquer sin, death, and the grave, He will empower us to do likewise when we turn from our lukewarm Christianity and awake to righteousness!

Chapter 8

Sign: Political Correctness

> And when they had brought them, they set them before the council: and the high priest asked them, Saying, Did not we straitly command you that ye should not teach in this name? and, behold, ye have filled Jerusalem with your doctrine, and intend to bring this man's blood upon us. Then Peter and the other apostles answered and said, We ought to obey God rather than men (Acts 5:27–29).

FOR A CHRISTIAN TO be politically correct in today's society, we must obey man rather than God. We may be American and patriotic, but first and foremost, we are to be a Christian and devoted to Jesus Christ.

This chapter is meant to focus on what political correctness is all about and how Christians should not be politically correct. If we are partakers of its beliefs, we are denying Christ.

When Bill Clinton ran for office, he said he wanted to give us "a government that looks more like America." Yet, with people like Donna Shalala, Roberta Achtenberg, Jocelyn Elders, etc. as his choice for the highest offices in the federal government, makes us wonder where he developed his "America" from.

What is Political Correctness? It is, in fact, the depreciation of Biblical truths and the increase of secular humanism. Secular humanism is a philosophy or life stance that embraces human reason, secular ethics, and philosophical naturalism while specifically rejecting religious doctrine. It believes humanity is capable of morality and self-fulfillment without belief in God.

According to George Gallup, in the 1960's, 67 percent of all Americans believed the Bible to be the actual word of God. In the seventies and eighties the number dropped to 37 percent. In 2017, only 24 percent believe it to be the actual word of God.

In 1892, after an extensive review of definitive documents of government, the justices declared, "this is a religious people. . . a Christian nation." In 1931, Justice George Sutherland handed down a ruling affirming we are a "Christian people." Justice William O. Douglas in 1952, ruled "we are a religious people and our institutions presuppose a Supreme Being."

What an incredible legacy. Yet, only ten years later, on June 25, 1962, the Supreme Court ruled in Engel v. Vitale that Bible reading was no longer legal in the public schools of this nation. Then, to add to this spiritual decline, on June 17, 1963, in Murray v. Curlett, the court stripped students in the public schools of their right to pray.

Our founding fathers knew and believed in the Bible. They knew only by God's consent could government govern, and individuals were first after God. This was to be a government of law, not of men. It was to be laws based on the laws of God alone.

Such a government rested squarely on Biblical principles and was limited by the inherent rights of those governed (we the people). These rights were to be those spelled out in the Scriptures. It's the right of man to be in obedience to the laws of God.

Laws are not made for a righteous man, but for the lawless and disobedient, for the ungodly and for sinners (1 Timothy 1:9). The purpose of laws is to punish the rebellious.

The decline in the literal translation of the Bible has caused the most dramatic changes in religious beliefs. Most of the teens today believe the Bible is nothing more than an ancient book of fables, legends, history, and moral teachings recorded by man. The majority of adults think most of Scripture must be interpreted figuratively (nonliterally) and not literally (actually).

To add fire to the fuel of this liberal mentality, the Jesus Seminar active in the 1980's, 1990's, and early 21st Century radically revised the New Testament to reflect what they believed is a more accurate account of the origins of Christianity. This panel, consisting of fifty critical Biblical scholars and one-hundred laymen, declared that only a fraction of the words attributed to Jesus were actually spoken by him.

> And if any man shall take away from the words of the book of this prophecy, God shall take away his part out of the book of life, and out of the holy city, and from the things which are written in this book (Revelation 22:19).

God's soldiers must not be swayed by so-called scholars, ministers, etc. who claim the Bible is not to be taken literally. Political correctness is a doctrine of devils and will lead all who are beguiled by its teaching to Hell.

If we look at history, the first schools in America were Christian home schools. By the 1630's, Puritans were founding schools to spread the Christian faith. On April 23, 1635, the first public school in what would become the United States was established in Boston, Massachusetts. Its schoolmaster was Philemon Pormont, a Puritan settler. In other words, the educational institutions were Christian schools, founded and operated by Christians mostly through voluntary association with local churches.

In these schools, the primary text was the Bible. The purpose was to educate children to become devout men and women of faith in Jesus Christ.

In 1857, a group of prominent American educators founded a professional association for teachers known as the National Education Association (NEA), and for many years was just that. It had little impact until the 1960's. At this time, it was allowed to force teachers to join or lose their jobs.

Today it is controlled by radicals with a definite political and social agenda. It's an agenda of secular humanism, socialism, and globalism. This is far different from what our forefathers declared the educational system was to accomplish.

The NEA uses the educational system to advance a radical liberal, social, and political agenda. It promotes free sex education, moral relativism, homosexuality as an alternative lifestyle, abortion, transgender (what you decide to be and not what God created you as), the removal of religious references from history books, etc.

As a result, core subjects like math, reading, and science, not to mention Christian principles are neglected. By removing prayer, the Bible, and the Ten Commandments, America has replaced them with drugs, condoms, immorality, etc.

> Woe unto them that call evil good, and good evil; that put darkness for light, and light for darkness; that put bitter for sweet, and sweet for bitter! Woe unto them that are wise in their own eyes, and prudent in their own sight! . . .Which justify the wicked for reward, and take away the righteousness of the righteous from him? Therefore as the fire devoureth the stubble, and the flame consumeth the chaff, so their root shall be as rottenness, and their blossom shall go up as dust: because they have cast away the law of the Lord of hosts, and despised the word of the Holy One of Israel (Isaiah 5:20–21, 23–24).

Our society has chosen to exalt sin and call immorality and perversion true virtue and commendable freedom. At the same time, it opposes righteousness by describing it as evil. When professing Christians join in this mentality, the flame will consume them like chaff because they have cast away the law of the Lord.

When Bill Clinton was president, he called sexual perversion such as homosexuality and lesbianism a legitimate alternative lifestyle that should be openly accepted.

God's soldiers opposing and accepting Biblical standards of sexual morality are called bigots who perpetuate oppressive prejudice. Pro-abortion advocates are called "sensitive" individuals with a deep commitment to the rights of women, while active pro-life supporters are called "extremists" or "religious fanatics." Lately, one of the pro-abortion Democrats running for president claimed that abortion should matter to everyone because women are people. That's how debased this country has come when it doesn't consider a baby to be a person.

America is undergoing a profound social crisis, and many pretend it isn't happening. Charles Colson wrote in a publication: "Belief in the Bible has declined, and religious influence has been so thoroughly scrubbed from public life that any honest observer would have to regard this as a post-Christian culture."

Unrighteousness in the church is seen in various news articles, such as: Adultery, financial-mismanagement accusations leveled at such and such ministry. In 1992, the Salem Religious Leaders Association officially welcomed a high priest witch into its ranks. Randal Wilkinson, priest at Saint Peter's Episcopal Church claimed that no one in the interfaith clergy support group could think of any compelling reason to forbid Poirer from joining.

> Regard not them that have familiar spirits, neither seek after wizards, to be defiled by them: I (am) the LORD your God (Leviticus 19:31).

> And the soul that turneth after such as have familiar spirits, and after wizards, to go a whoring after them, I will even set my face against that soul, and will cut him off from among his people (Leviticus 20:6).

How many Christians go to fortune tellers, psychics, follow their horoscopes, etc. for direction and ignore the word of God? How many seek the counsel of those who are false ministers? How many fellowship with lukewarm Christians?

It was no surprise when the church voted for a second term for Clinton hoping to bring on the "rapture." Instead of fighting the corruption in our nation, they chose an escapism mentality. Yes, we are to look for the blessed hope (Christ's return) but not with the attitude of "get me out of this mess."

Instead of coming against the political correctness agenda of secular humanism, socialism, globalism, and rejection of the God of the Bible, many seem to be joining in its mentality. If it's not joined, it seems to be ignored by professing Christians who continue to sit in their seat of do nothing and allow its corruption to spread like leaven to contaminate the whole country.

It's because of the church's compromise that America has reached such a spiritual decline. Now, many in the church want to hold hands with fornicators, adulterers, homosexuals, etc. This is not going to prepare the church or anyone for the return of Christ. The church must wake up.

Through the power of prayer, God's soldiers are supposed to bind the powers of Hell and loose the powers of Heaven (Matthew 18:18). When we bind something, we are not to tie ourselves up with it. Too many are now entangled in sins that were bound.

Prayerfully, this chapter has awakened righteousness in those who were compromising and leaning toward political correctness. Christian, we are supposed be the wall that separates the world from the church. It's us who must push back the gates of Hell and expose the corruption, socialism, globalism, immorality, and the anti-God mentality political correctness is built upon!

Chapter 9

Sign: Spiritual Blindness

The burden which Habakkuk the prophet did see. O Lord, how long shall I cry, and thou wilt not hear!. . . and there are that raise up strife and contention. Therefore the law is slacked, and judgment doth never go forth: for the wicked doth compass about the righteous; therefore wrong judgment proceedeth (Habakkuk 1:1–4).

THIS CHAPTER IS MEANT to illuminate the neglect of the "Religious Right" and our compromise and lukewarm stance against what is evil. Lukewarm Christianity results in spiritual blindness. If we allow the scales to fall from our eyes, we will see a lack of rectitude or righteousness is the result of becoming lukewarm in what we believe.

To be religious is to be pious, godly, to have a love and reverence for the Supreme Being, and to obey his precepts.

To be considered right refers to morals and religion. It means to be just according to the standard of truth and justice or the will of God. That alone is right in the sight of God, which is in harmony to his will and the only perfect standard of truth and justice.

In social and political affairs, right is in harmony with the laws and customs of a country, provided the laws and customs are not repugnant (opposite, contrary) to the laws of God. In the literal sense, right is a straight line of conduct, and wrong is a crooked one.

Right, therefore, is a righteousness or straightness, and perfect rectitude is found only in an infinite Being and his will. The more nearly the righteousness of God's soldier approaches to the standard of God's divine law, the more exalted and dignified is our character.

On the other hand, wrong is the absence of moral rightness. It is deviation from the line of righteousness prescribed by God. This digression causes us to be wrong or improper, to be erroneous, to possess unethical ideas, and to travel a wrong way of life.

With the definitions given of religious, right, and wrong, it would seem that the "Religious Right" is correct. This is especially true when rectitude (true straightness) is measured in the will of God, and wrong is contingent on being out of the will of God. Yet, careful consideration of the rectitude (straightness) of the "Religious Right" brings us to our Scripture reference in Habakkuk.

The prophet had been praying for God to stop the wrong he saw oppressing the covenant people. However, it appeared as if God was doing nothing but tolerating violence, injustice, and the destruction of his law. Habakkuk was shocked (as is today's true disciples of Christ) that God is punishing the sin of his people with a people (the liberal left, etc.) who do not even try to obey the law of God.

Wickedness appears to go on without penalty, and the punishment deserved is deferred. The law of God, the whole law, moral, judicial, etc. is slacked (weakened, little studied, and less obeyed by most). As for judgment, not only private men neglect the law (of God), but magistrates, judges, public officers, etc. pervert, prevent, or obstruct it.

The unjust and violent compasses about our Nation as if it is besieged, with the design to oppress and ruin by false witness, ungodliness, and bribery. Wrong judgment condemns the innocent and acquits the guilty.

Because the evil pays no attention to God's law, it seems to have lost all its restraining and correcting power. The law of God appears to be powerless against the wicked. His law is not carried out and right judgment is not pronounced.

Now, the righteous complain in vain that we are grievously oppressed by the wicked and those in power and authority. The wicked authoritarians, who are breakers of God's law, cry that "evil is good and good is evil," and prevail. Seemingly, the pro-abortionists, pro-homosexuals, pro-humanists, etc. are considered right in their protesting. Even some of the past presidents in the white house were on the side of the breakers of God's law.

What is wrong with the "Religious Right?" Why do the breakers of the commandments of God seem to be prospering? The answer is simply this, as in Habakkuk's day, God is using the ruthless and ungodly Babylonians (those opposing God's soldiers) to come against the "Religious Right."

Judah's rectitude was lacking, and the "Religious Right" is lacking in righteousness. The standards of God are deficient in the lives of much of Christianity. Many of us do not have a biblical foundation for our particular belief. Some are not sure if abortion is actually murder, if homosexuality is an alternative lifestyle, if the alcoholic and drug addict is sick, etc. As there was sin in Judah, there is sin in the "Religious Right."

> I know thy works, that thou art neither cold nor hot: I would thou wert cold or hot. So then because thou art lukewarm, and neither cold nor hot, I will spew thee out of my mouth. Because thou sayest, I am rich, and increased with goods, and have need of nothing; and knowest not that thou are wretched, and miserable, and poor, and blind, and naked: I counsel thee to buy of me gold tried in the fire, that thou mayest be rich; and white raiment, that thou mayest be clothed, and that the shame of thy nakedness do not appear; and anoint thine eyes with eyesalve that thou mayest see (Revelation 3:15–18).

The root sin is described in the above verses. Is the "Religious Right" hot or cold in its beliefs? What is the statement of faith upon which it claims to be the right? Is any statement of faith strongly proclaimed? Is our goal to exalt Jesus, some elite members, the Republican Party, etc.?

How can we claim to be the "Religious Right" without a definitive biblical mandate? We may take the anti-abortion, anti-homosexual, or anti-humanists, etc. stance. However, if we are ignorant and unlearned in the Scriptures, we are really nothing more than a self-righteous bigot.

It's not enough to say we are part of the "Religious Right." We must proclaim with biblical reasons why we believe what we believe. Again, this is why doctrine is of the utmost importance. It is imperative to have a knowledge of Scripture.

Our viewpoint holds no weight. It's God's declaration we must stand upon. In order for the ignorant of God's word to comprehend that God takes the anti-abortion, anti-homosexual, anti-humanism, etc. position, the word of God must be administered full strength. Diluting the prescription will never heal any sickness or disease, and a watered down dosage of God's word will never heal the sin sick soul.

In order to know what God calls right and wrong, the Bible must be proclaimed as our grounds as to why we believe what we believe. It is in the Scriptures where the mind of God (his view of things) is found. Every facet of life must be viewed in light of or in view of God's word.

> Behold, the day of the Lord cometh, cruel both with wrath and fierce anger, to lay the land desolate: and he shall destroy the sinners thereof out of it (Isaiah 13:9).

Much is spoken concerning God's love. However, Isaiah exposes He is also a righteous God who emphatically hates sin and punishes all who insist on transgressing his word.

Let me explain some of the lukewarm mentality or lack of righteousness in the "Religious Right." If we believe that abortion is murder, but believe that homosexuality is a birth defect, or the drunkard is sick reveals a lack of rectitude or righteousness.

> Thou shalt not lie with mankind, as with womankind: it is abomination (Leviticus 18:22).

> Even as Sodom and Gomorrah, and the cities about them in like manner, giving themselves over to fornication, and going after strange flesh, are set forth for an example, suffering the vengeance of eternal fire (Jude 7).

According to God's word, it's sin. God does not try to pacify the sinner. He calls homosexuality an abomination. One of the reasons for the destruction of Sodom and Gomorrah was its sin of homosexuality (Genesis 19:5–7; 2 Peter 2:6).

Scripture clearly declares that the homosexual, drunkard, murderer (abortionist), etc. will not enter the Kingdom of God (1 Corinthians 6:9–11; Revelation 21:8).

Although some of the "Religious Right" are knowledgeable in the Scriptures, many are utterly ignorant of its implication. Their knowledge is merely superficial or lukewarm. God demands propagation of his word. It's his will for all be saved and have a knowledge of the truth (1 Timothy 2:4).

God wants the wicked to know why they are considered wicked in his eyes. He wants all to know what his word calls sin. It's not a matter of what the "Religious Right" believes. It's what God says about the belief that's critical.

Are our beliefs founded on the word of God? Can we trace our convictions to the word of God? Just to claim we believe gays should be restricted from our military, appears to be nothing more than a personal preference. When in actuality, it is a biblical mandate. To accept homosexuality is to accept sin, and to accept sin is to reject God.

The lack of a solid biblical gauge is the wrong that overshadows the "Religious Right." Although we take the right stand with God, do we know why we do? Are we here because we don't want to be named with the left? Do we agree with what the "Religious Right" is supposed to believe?

It seems to avoid division in the ranks, we proclaim no definitive mandate. There's so much diversity of beliefs. Some align with God's word, while others resist his word. Christ is not diverse in what He believes. His measuring rod is his word. God measures what we believe through his word. There is no grey area in God's word concerning sin, it's black or white. To be grey in what we believe is to be lukewarm.

As the "Religious Right," we are the wall that must stand against the evil invading our country. Our lukewarm Christianity has allowed unrighteousness to erode the righteousness in our nation. Because of this, God has been using the unrighteous to overtake us as He did to Judah. However, if we accept the truth of God's word, the scales will fall from our eyes, our spiritual blindness will be healed, and we'll blaze the light of his word on the darkness overtaking our Nation!

Chapter 10

Sign: Defection

> Now the Spirit speaketh expressly, that in the latter times
> some shall depart from the faith; giving heed to seducing
> spirits, and doctrines of devils; speaking lies in hypoc-
> risy; having their conscience seared with a hot iron (1
> Timothy 4:1).

THIS CHAPTER WAS INSPIRED by the former ministers, worship leaders, song writers, etc. who have recently defected from the faith. Some have gone shipwreck and are mocking former beliefs. Before that, there were claims of a mega preacher who allegedly sought out a hitman to murder someone.

In recent times, a mega-church pastor announced he'd left his wife and the Christian faith. A few days later, he posted pictures of himself at a gay pride event. However, he's not the first high-profile minister to apostatize. It seems a worship leader, who wrote many songs for the Christian faith has renounced his beliefs. Another well-known Christian artist who wrote and sang such inspiring songs has left his family and states homosexuality is approved by God.

The heart wrenching part is that some are actually proud to be called apostates. One of the defectors has started a podcast about the journey. He's delighted he's no longer a Christian. There have been others, but this is enough for what this chapter is teaching.

In our Scripture text, the Holy Spirit is clearly warning that during the end times, many will depart (this means to fall away), apostatize, defect from the faith. Some will claim the individuals were never saved. However, how can we depart (fall away) from something we were not part of?

According to the British English definition, if something falls away, it breaks off from the thing it was fixed to. An example is: "Plaster was falling away from the walls." The plaster is part of the wall, it was one with the wall.

> Men and brethren, this scripture must needs have been fulfilled, which the Holy Ghost by the mouth of David spake before concerning Judas, which was guide to them that took Jesus. For he was numbered with us, and had obtained part of this ministry. . . That he may take part of this ministry and apostleship, from which Judas by transgression fell, that he might go to his own place (Acts 1:16,17,25).

Now, Matthew 10:1–4 declares Jesus called the twelve. It's Jesus who calls to the ministry after we become his disciple (Ephesians 4:11–12). Judas fell away or defected from the faith, because of his lack of self-denial.

> And he said to them all, If any man will come after me, let him deny himself, and take up his cross daily, and follow me (Luke 9:23).

A careful inspection will reveal if we leave the faith (apostatize), we have done so because we neglected the basics of keeping the conviction. The first and most important criteria is to deny self its lust of the flesh, lust of the eyes, and the pride of life.

I believe some may think the person is backsliding. Let me interject that an apostate (one who falls away) is not a backslider. A backslider is a person who turns away from his Christian faith for a season for whatever reason. This is seen in Peter who denies Christ, but after he weeps bitterly in repentance (Luke 22:61–62) is restored to a right relationship with Christ. Whereas, the apostate is explained in Chapter six concerning those who are twice dead. An apostate has reached the point of no return, for he refused to deny self and remain in Christ. There's no restoration for those who are dead and have been plucked up by the roots. However, ONLY God knows the difference between the backslider and the apostate.

To deny self is to literally pick up our cross daily and follow Jesus no matter how severe the storm, how impossible the obstacle seems to be, how deceptive Satan's strategies are, etc. We can't deny self today and indulge it tomorrow. It's a life-time of self-sacrifice and self-denial. It's a constant squeezing of our fleshly appetites to remain in the straight and narrow path that will always make our flesh uncomfortable.

> Be not deceived; God is not mocked: for whatsoever a man soweth, that shall he also reap. For he that soweth to his flesh shall of the flesh reap corruption; but he that soweth to the Spirit shall of the Spirit reap life everlasting (Galatians 6:7–8).

Too many are becoming weary in their well-doing and will reap the consequences of their sin. What we sow is what we reap. Yes, denying self, taking up our cross daily, and following Jesus seems like a long arduous journey at times. But if we neglect our spiritual health here, Hell is eternal.

1 Timothy is forewarning God's soldiers who were once gifted and empowered to preach the message of Christ effectively will fall from the faith. We see it happening. They're defecting from the faith because the straight and narrow is too confining on their flesh.

Once we start on the road of self-indulgence instead of self-denial, we give into the deception and enticement of evil spirits. We become lukewarm and the deception of false teachers is accepted as truth. As I revealed in my book, *Spiritual Shipwreck on the Horizon: Exhorting Christians to Contend for the Faith and Comprehend the Deceitfulness of Sin*, some are convinced they can say a sinner's prayer, then live in sins that will not inherit the kingdom of God, and still go to Heaven.

> And you, that were sometime alienated and enemies in your mind by wicked works, yet now hath he reconciled in the body of his flesh through death, to present you holy and unblameable and unreproveable in his sight: IF ye continue in the faith grounded and settled, and be not

> moved away from the hope of the gospel, which ye have
> heard, and which was preached to every creature which
> is under heaven; whereof I Paul am made a minster
> (Colossians 1:21–23).

With a lack of self-denial, many become lukewarm. The Scripture text above makes evident we are only going to be presented holy, unblameable, and unreproveable IF we remain steadfast and unmoveable in the faith of the gospel. We must actively yield to the Holy Spirit at all times. As soon as we give place or yield to our flesh, we begin a downward spiral into lukewarm Christianity. If not terminated, it will lead to our defecting (apostatizing) from the faith all together.

Defection will be at a high in the latter times because sound doctrine will be overlooked, and self-denial will be disregarded by many claiming to be Christians. Only through a knowledge of God's word will the signs of lukewarm Christianity that leads to desertion be recognized. Scripture is our source guiding us to correct behavior or moral living, whereas, unsound doctrine will produce sinful behavior or immoral living.

It's imperative we are not moved from the hope of the gospel. This means we must not return to our former life of sin, hopelessness, and spiritual destruction apart from Christ. Because of the leaving or questioning the hope of the gospel, some of God's soldiers will abandon the faith. Our love of truth is no longer worth the negativity we receive from those who oppose truth. We get tired of self-denial, picking up the heavy cross of ridicule, storms, obstacles, trials, etc. and start travelling down the wide and broad path.

This is not done overnight. It's allowing a little compromise (leaven of the world) into our life. As we ignore the conviction of the Holy Spirit, we allow a little more compromise (leaven of the world). Before we know it, we are walking in the lust of the flesh, the lust of the eyes, and the pride of life. We are no longer doers of the word, but hearers only who have deceived ourselves (James 1:22). We no longer contend for the faith, and are content on the wide and broad way. Deception has completely engulfed us, and we are beguiled into believing we are still Christians.

Let me interject a personal story that happened when I was young in the Lord. There was a Christmas Party at the church, and we were supposed to dress up as Bible characters. As I was sitting there, a woman about my age came over to me. She always had her entourage of young men who followed her. Anyway, she said, "Ah, Mary Magdalene." I shook my head and said, "No, it's Mary of Bethany." She chuckled and looked at the young men and said, "How long have you been saved?" I said about nine months. At that she looked at the young men, laughed, and said, "I've been saved over five years, I could carry you." At that they all laughed and walked away. As they walked away, one of the deacons came over to me. He patted my hand and said, "Rita, anyone can claim to be a Christian, but that doesn't mean they read the Bible. A knowledge of the word of God reveals if you are what you claim to be. According to God's word, it's quite obvious that you are Mary of Bethany."

Without a knowledge of the truth of the Bible, people will believe what they are told. Those young men believed her. It's apparent she received her knowledge from watching a Hollywood movie and NOT from the word of God. Because of the departure from Bible truth, unbiblical teaching is widely being propagated and accepted by Christians who once claimed they would die for the faith. Now, staunch believers are dying to the faith. God's soldiers are defecting from Christianity by bringing in doctrines that make null and void biblical faith. Because the tenets of faith are no longer believed, a compromising and flesh appealing gospel is widely accepted and followed.

We must recognize the individuals with great charisma and God-given ability can be deceived because of their lack of self-denial. As they are deceived, they will deceive others (2 Timothy 3:13).

Our protection against yielding to seducing spirits that lead to lukewarm Christianity is to have complete dependence on and total loyalty to God and his word with unwavering faith. Only as we deny self, decrease, and allow him to increase will we remain steadfast, unmoveable, always abounding in the work of the Lord, and avoid defection!

Chapter 11

Sign: Itching Ears

> I charge thee therefore before God, and the Lord Jesus
> Christ, who shall judge the quick and the dead at his
> appearing and his kingdom; preach the word; be instant
> in season, out of season; reprove, rebuke, exhort with all
> longsuffering and doctrine. For the time will come when
> they will not endure sound doctrine; but after their own
> lusts shall heap to themselves teachers, having itching
> ears; and they shall turn away their ears from the truth,
> and shall be turned unto fables. But watch thou in all
> things, endure afflictions, do the work of an evangelist,
> make full proof of thy ministry (2 Timothy 4:1–5).

THESE VERSES IN TIMOTHY, are informing us how lukewarm Christianity will be recognized. Because of indulging our own lusts and
not denying self, we will shun truth and accept teachers of itching
ears or what is easy on the flesh. We will no longer listen to the
word of God that renounces sin, warns of the consequences of sin,
or talks about the baptism of fire to cleanse sin.

Paul is warning Timothy of the importance of preaching the
word. He was to be ready in any situation to give proper doctrine
concerning Christ's crucifixion for the sins of the world. He had
to be prepared to give the word whether of rebuke, correction, or
encouragement.

If we become slack on reflecting the truth of the gospel, we
could easily begin to question what we believe. Satan wants us to

think we lack love, or we would not be so adamant about sin. He badgers us until we wonder if the homosexual was actually born that way, was the person actually born a woman inside a man's body, was the person actually born a man inside a woman's body, is the alcoholic actually sick. We begin to question what the Bible says as truth.

In the beginning, God created mankind as male and female (Mark 10:6; Genesis 1:27). Our anatomy is what sex we were born. To believe otherwise is either demon possession or a spirit of confusion. Neither are of God, but the devil. Furthermore, Scripture is clear about God's sentiments about homosexuality. Romans 1:25–28 divulges that because of their refusal to keep God in their knowledge and their rebellion against truth, God gave them over to a reprobate, degenerate, corrupted, polluted, contaminated mind.

All of God's soldiers must be equipped with the necessary word in any situation we might encounter. We need to be ready with the Scriptures (our sword of the Spirit) to give the reason of the hope that is in us. Only the word of God is the wherewith to answer whoever reproaches us (Psalm 119:42).

Without studying the word of God, we will not rightly divide Scriptures, or have a knowledge of sound doctrine. We are only workmen approved by God when we know how to wield our sword or the word of God (2 Timothy 2:15) and cut to pieces the lies of the devil and his advocates.

A knowledge of church history reveals there have always been some of God's soldiers who refuse to listen to or support teachings that oppose selfish and sinful behavior. However, as we see the day of the Lord approaching, lukewarm Christianity, which results in defiance of God's word and acceptance of deception, will grow at an alarming rate.

There will be claims of Christianity, but they will not endure sound doctrine. They will have a form of godliness but deny its power. In other words, they will not tolerate faith that emphasizes Holy Spirit power, his call to moral purity, and separation from the world with its ungodly way of life. Instead, lukewarm Christianity will seek out teachers of itching ears who preach a watered down or diluted gospel to pamper or encourage sinful desires.

Professing Christians will turn away their ears from the truth. We see this deception becoming a daily reality. Many are no longer tolerating sound Bible doctrine preaching that boldly defends the truth and takes a firm stand against sin. Those who stand against sin are persecuted, ridiculed, mocked, and called haters of mankind, etc.

It seems one foot in Christianity and one foot in the world is the gospel being sought out. However, lukewarm Christianity is utterly unacceptable to Christ. He will spue us out of his mouth. I mean, He died for us to overcome this life. The overcoming is conquering the power of sin in our life.

I remember when I first heard a homosexual proclaim he's still a Christian who is finally living his life the way God created him. God did not create anyone a homosexual, the lust of man's/woman's flesh created such wicked behavior. Scripture makes evident that those who commit the abomination of going after strange flesh (homosexuality) are set forth for as an example of suffering the vengeance of eternal fire or Hell (Jude 7).

As I mentioned in my book, *Spiritual Shipwreck on the Horizon: Exhorting Christians to Contend for the Faith and Comprehend the Deceitfulness of Sin*, deception does not happen overnight. It's like a drip of water that keeps dripping until it becomes a puddle, then a pool, then a lake, and then an ocean. Leaven starts off microscopic until it has leavened or corrupted the whole. If we allow a little leaven of lethargy, compromise, or seduction in our life to go unchecked, we will eventually become completely contaminated.

When we sit in the sun, we don't get sunburned right away. It's only after we have lingered in the sun for too long that we become burned. If we entertain a little leaven without nipping it in the bud, it will grow until it has consumed us with its deception.

How many are seeking out pastors, teachers, etc. who are eloquent and entertaining speakers, who preach messages to reassure us that we can live in sin and remain a Christian when God's word clearly states the opposite?

Itching ear preaching is sought after by God's soldiers who no longer want to keep oppressing (denying) our flesh on the straight and narrow way. We start off by dabbing our foot in the murky water of the world. Then when we have convinced ourselves this isn't too bad, we step in with both feet. Before long, we are immersed in the so-called pleasures of this world, are no longer convicted by the Holy Spirit, and are on the broad and wide way leading to Hell.

Paul warns that we had better be prepared to endure afflictions if we are to live for Christ and uphold the truth of Scripture. If we're standing firm for the faith, we must expect to be ridiculed, ostracized, mocked, hated, called names, etc. This is because many are turned unto fables, stories, tales, myths, etc. and are accepting anything and everything that encourages fleshly behavior.

Make no mistake about it, if we remain faithful to God and his word, we had better expect persecution and suffering for our faith. We must separate from churches, people, ministers, etc. who claim to be Christians, but deny Christ in their life. The false teachers compromise the truth of Scripture to tickle the ears (fleshly appetites) of their hearers.

> And every one that heareth these sayings of mine, and doeth them not, shall be likened unto a foolish man, which built his house upon the sand: And the rain descended, and the floods came, and the winds blew, and beat upon that house; and it fell: and great was the fall of it (Matthew 7:26–27).

There are Christians who base what is believed on new revelations, miracles, success, human-based goals that are unbiblical. Any unscriptural belief is building our house upon the sand that will cause a great fall and the destruction of our faith. If a foundation is shakable or capable of being weakened, it will sooner or later collapse. This truth is expounded at length in my book, *Storms Are Faith's Workout: Preparing Christians for Spiritual Ambush.*

> Watch and pray; that ye enter not into temptation: the spirit indeed is willing, but the flesh is weak (Matthew 26:41).

We must never abandon our commitment to the faith. Any wavering can give way to temptation of the flesh. If we can't endure a little fatigue when there is no affliction, what will we do when the trial of our fleshly appetites is upon us. Will we deny self or yield to its desires?

To be enabled to stand against the trials of our flesh, we need to know how to use the full armor of God. For an understanding of its use, I suggest you read my book: *Faith's Journey Confronts Obstacles: Instructing God's Soldiers to Overcome in His Armor.*

Only a life of denying self its lusts will keep us from becoming part of lukewarm Christianity. As we study the Scriptures, decrease and allow him to increase, stand fully armed and proficient in God's armor, itching ear teachers will be recognized and rejected!

Chapter 12

Sign: Deception Accepted

Now we beseech you, brethren, by the coming of our Lord Jesus Christ, and by our GATHERING TOGETHER unto him, that ye be not soon shaken in mind, or be troubled, neither by spirit, nor by word, nor by letter as from us, as that the day of Christ is at hand. Let no man DECEIVE you by any means: for that day shall not come, except there come a falling away first, and that man of sin be revealed, the son of perdition; who opposeth and exalteth himself above all that is called God, or that is worshipped; so that he as God sitteth in the temple of God, shewing himself that he is God (2 Thessalonians 2:1–4).

IT's MY PRAYER THE deception overtaking much of Christianity will be illuminated allowing the scales to fall from the eyes of many who have been deceived by false doctrines and erroneous teachings. I believe this chapter will reveal a profound truth that's not being taught by many. Instead, many are watching for false indicators that have deceived us into believing a lie.

What does the apostle mean when he says our gathering together unto him? According to Merriam Webster it's to bring together in one body or place. It means to collect, congregate, pick up; to catch or collect. Now, what does the word rapture suggest? It's the bringing together in one place, to pick up, to catch or collect, or to be caught up with the Lord in the clouds.

I'm not denying there will be a rapture or gathering together with the Lord. My concern is the escapism mentality has too many of God's soldiers in never-never land, a place outside of the reality of Scripture. I can't count the times I've heard Christians claiming we'll be out of this mess soon. They claim to almost hear the sound of the trump. That mentality is not contending for the faith. It's not standing against the evil overtaking our country, we've become lukewarm Christianity lacking a zeal for righteousness. Many are not contending for the faith and have become wishy-washy or anemic in their doctrine or what they believe.

Such mentality has God's soldiers so engrossed looking for the rapture, that we are neglecting our warfare. When this occurs, we begin to slip from our steadfastness into a complacent, compromising state that's looking for a way out. I call it the escapism mentality from reality. That's what the alcoholic, drug addict, etc. does. Rather than deny or fight our flesh, we look for a way to pamper it.

I mean, really, how many of the early Christians would have stood against such persecution with today's lukewarm Christianity mindset? Those believers suffered horrendous persecution at the hands of Roman emperors. We seem to want our Christian walk to be a tip-toe through the tulips. Marshmallow saints will not overcome this life, for such will never endure persecution at that level.

Yes, we'll not suffer the wrath of God if we overcome this life (1 Thessalonians 5:9). However, the bowls of wrath are not poured out until after the abomination of desolation spoken by the prophet Daniel (Daniel 9:27; Matthew 24:15). The anti-Christ will sit in the temple and claim to be God before the bowls of wrath are poured out. Furthermore, God's final wrath is Hell.

Paul was aware of the signs before our gathering together (rapture) to be with the Lord. It's obvious by his speech that he wasn't sure if he would be here to see the anti-Christ sit in the temple proclaiming he is God.

Listen to me, Paul is teaching that before we are gathered together or raptured, we will witness the anti-Christ sitting in the Holy Temple claiming to be God? If he thought he would be here, how do we assume we'll be raptured away before?

Hear me, many will fall away before the man of sin claims to be God. What I am trying to convey is the falling away will be many of those who were looking to be raptured before the tribulation. Their lukewarm and marshmallow Christianity did not prepare them for this. In other words, because of compromise and lack of self-denial, God's soldiers did not keep up with the footmen in a time of peace (Jeremiah 12:5). When things get tough (contending with horses and the swelling of Jordan), we will not contend for the faith. It's like the Israelites in the wilderness who lost faith in the God who miraculously delivered them from Egyptian bondage and feared to go into the Promised Land because of the giants and walled cities (Numbers 13:26–14:10). When it came time to deny their flesh and fight the good fight of faith, they gave into their flesh.

If God's soldiers want to overcome this life. It is essential to put our flesh under and read to the end of this book. Many are not aware of the signs of the time, and are not accurately interpreting or rightly dividing them. Because of this, we are accepting what is taught by man and not revelation of the Scriptures from the Holy Spirit.

Christianity has become deceived through a lack of warfare. We don't want to fight our flesh to be righteous, holy, and godly. Let's face it, how many believe the sinner's prayer is a ticket to Heaven and indulge in the sin's that will not inherit the kingdom of God? This mentality has many stagnant in our warfare against the enemy destroying our faith? How many of us will go hungry or without and not take the mark? If we are falling prey to false doctrines to pamper our flesh and its desires now, do we really think we'll not yield to the mark?

I know this chapter is a difficult one, but God's soldiers must awake to righteousness and sin not. If an awakening does not take place, we'll be carried away by the deceptive measures of Satan and be part of the falling away.

> Behold, I shew you a mystery: We shall not all sleep, but we shall all be changed, in a moment, in the twinkling of an eye, at the last trump: for the trumpet shall sound, and the dead shall be raised incorruptible, and we shall be changed (1 Corinthians 15:51–52).

> For the Lord himself shall descend from heaven with a shout, with the voice of the archangel, and with the trump of God: and the dead in Christ shall rise first: then we which are alive and remain shall be caught up together with them in the clouds, to meet the Lord in the air: and so shall we ever be with the Lord (1 Thessalonians 4:16–17).

Where in the Scriptures does it claim the tribulation saints who lose their lives are not part of the dead in Christ who will be raised first? I can't find such in my Bible. If we're in Christ, we're in Christ whether Old Testament saints or New Testament saints. Tribulation saints are part of the New Testament saints. No different than the early Christians who suffered such persecution were part of the New Testament saints. Furthermore, Revelation 6:9 says: "And when he had opened the fifth seal, I saw under the altar the souls of them that were slain for the word of God, and for the testimony which they held." The saints who were martyred throughout the ages are included there. It is the souls of all who have died for the faith of Jesus Christ.

What I am trying to communicate is the dead in Christ are ALL who have believed in Christ the Messiah (whether in his coming or that He came), and died in that faith. We don't separate the Old Testament saints from the New Testament saints. The saints of the New Testament are also the tribulation saints. Let me clarify this. It is Old Testament believers and New Testament believers. We cannot separate the tribulation saints as another category. Christ's death on the cross brought together both Jew and Greek. He broke down the middle wall of petition making both Jew and Gentile one new man in Christ allowing both to have access by one Spirit unto the Father (Ephesians 2:14–18).

No matter what time in the New Testament dispensation we die in Christ, it's all the dead in Christ who shall rise first. There are not two raptures or gathering together with Christ. Paul makes this fact clear. The gathering together (rapture) will NOT take place until the falling away and after the anti-Christ sits in the Temple and claims to be God.

Don't get me wrong, I also believed I would be out of here before the anti-Christ was revealed. I became born again in the Assemblies of God where my husband and I were Youth Leaders, pastored with the Church of God, and ordained with the Pentecostal Church of God where I pastored and worked as an evangelist.

I went non-denominational, because I could no longer sign a statement to only teach the pre-tribulation belief. In clear conscience, I had too many questions. Furthermore, how could I teach what I believed was not balanced in Scripture? Apparently, according to Paul's teaching, the gathering together with the Lord is after the anti-Christ sits in the Holy Temple as God.

He makes clear that we are not to be deceived by any man/woman into believing the gathering together or rapture will come before the falling away and the man of sin sits in the temple of God, professing to be God is revealed. Only lukewarm Christianity believes the fallacy that teaches against what Paul is clarifying to those who have eyes to see and ears to hear. Only deception will convince us to believe the opposite of what is stated in Scripture, because we are set on pampering our flesh.

> Thou therefore endure hardness, as a good soldier of Jesus Christ (2 Timothy 2:3).

Paul is entreating Timothy, that a soldier of Jesus Christ, is to endure, prevail, tolerate, withstand, suffer, brave, etc. hardness. God's soldiers are to overcome all suffering, trials, tribulations, storms, obstacles, etc. that come our way.

What that's saying to us is as a soldier must be willing to suffer because he/she desires to please his/her commanding officer. Born again believers are soldiers in the army of the Lord, we must be willing to suffer tribulations, troubles, sufferings, hardships, etc. We must not concentrate on our discomfort, but on pleasing our Lord (our commanding officer). Matthew 24:13 states, "But he that shall endure unto the end, the same shall be saved." We have not made it until we have lasted, continued, or remained to the end.

While many of God's soldiers are looking to be raptured, have quit reading the signs, are lulled in false beliefs, the devil and his hosts are destroying this One Nation Under God. Lukewarm

Christianity has become so lethargic that it's joined in the unrighteousness prevailing. Some have slipped back into what we were before meeting Jesus and are so deceived by false teachers and false doctrines to believe we can live in sin and still go to Heaven, or we're looking for the rapture before the falling away and the revealing of the man of sin (the anti-Christ). In other words, too many have the escapism from reality mentality.

> That in the dispensation of the fulness of times He might gather together in one all things in Christ, both which are in Heaven, and which are on earth; even Him (Ephesians 1:10).

When it is his time, all who are in Christ (dead in Heaven and alive on earth) will be gathered together (raptured) in Christ. In other words, ALL who are dead and ALL who are alive will be gathered together (raptured) at the same time. This is a one-time happening.

> For the Lord himself shall descend from heaven with a shout, with the voice of the archangel, and with the trump of God: and the dead in Christ shall rise first: Then we which are alive and remain shall be caught up together with them in the clouds, to meet the Lord in the air: and so shall we ever be with the Lord (1 Thessalonians 4:16–17).

Quit accepting deception and awaken out of slumber. There will only be one raising of the dead in Christ, not two. Those who are in Christ and die in the tribulation will be raised at the same time as all dead in Christ.

Paul is emphatically saying the coming of Christ, his return, the day of Christ will not come until the falling away and the man of sin (the anti-Christ) sits in the Temple and claims to be God. Our gathering together or the rapture will not happen before those signs are seen or fulfilled.

> Because thou hast kept the word of my patience, I also will keep thee from the hour of temptation, which shall come upon all the world, to try them that dwell upon the earth (Revelation 3:10).

This is an important Scripture that has been so misinterpreted and thus totally disregarding Paul's teaching about our gathering together with the Lord. The Lord is not claiming to take us out, but to keep (maintain, stabilize, withstand, hold up, etc.) us from the hour of temptation (adversity, hardship, difficulty, danger, etc.).

The early Christians suffered incredible torture at the hands of Nero and others, but God didn't take them out of it. They weren't marshmallow or lukewarm Christians, but warriors of faith. Furthermore, the Israelites, living in Goshen, were kept from most of the plagues in Egypt. The plagues in Revelation are not God's wrath any more than the Egyptian plagues and neither is the anti-Christ reign. Nero could be considered a type of anti-Christ at the persecution he imposed upon the early Christians. They were not pulled out because it would be uncomfortable on their flesh. Instead they endured unto the end. True soldiers of God don't look for a way out of trying times, but endure, persist, persevere, prevail to the end.

> But he, being full of the Holy Ghost, looked up steadfastly into heaven, and saw the glory of God, and Jesus standing on the right hand of God, And said, Behold, I see the heavens opened, and the Son of man standing on the right hand of God. . .And they stoned Stephen, calling upon God, and saying, Lord Jesus, receive my spirit (Acts 7:55–59).

This is another example of God keeping us during danger. Stephen was able to withstand incredible hardship and overcame victoriously in Christ. Marshmallow Christians or lukewarm Christianity will not be kept because they don't want to suffer (deny) their flesh.

That's why so many have the escapism mentality and are looking for the rapture before the fulness of times. Paul's teaching makes clear that it will not happen before the falling away and the anti-Christ sits in the Temple claiming to be God. That's why he warned about being deceived into believing it would occur before then. Soldier pay attention to signs. Incorrect reading can lead to wreckage.

What I'm trying to illuminate is we're only promised we won't suffer God's wrath. God's word doesn't promise we won't suffer false Christs, wars, tribulations, famines, plagues, death, the anti-Christ reign, and martyrdom spoken of in Revelation. If we overcome (endure, suffer, persist, survive) until the end (fullness of times), we will inherit all things (Revelation 21:7).

Lukewarm Christianity or marshmallow Christians are looking for a tip-toe through the tulips Christianity that doesn't exist. I'm reminded of Pliable, who in "Pilgrim's Progress," started on Faith's Journey with Christian, but soon turned back because of the hardships, trials, storms, obstacles, etc. that must be faced, endured, and overcome.

I opened this book with the Hale-Bopp comet and how it was a sign that was wrongly read. The misinterpretation or misreading was the destruction of a group who read or interpreted it erroneously. What I'm endeavoring to do here is to encourage God's soldiers to let the scales fall. It's imperative to study God's word about the end time. We have no idea when the tribulation will begin, but we have clear signs in the Scripture of what will take place before and after.

1. A major **sign** is revealed in Daniel 9:27 showing that when the anti-Christ signs a treaty with Israel for 7 years, we are in the beginning of the tribulation. That means when someone signs a peace treaty with Israel for 7 years, he is the anti-Christ, and we have begun the tribulation.

2. Matthew 24:3–31, the disciples ask for a **sign** of his coming. Jesus warns, **"Take heed that no man deceive you."** Then He reveals all the signs that will occur BEFORE his coming. Jesus is **not returning** until **after** the tribulation of those days. Pay attention that Jesus warns that man will deceive us.

3. Another **sign** of how the last days are recognized according to 2 Timothy 3, "This know also, that in the last days perilous times shall come. For men shall be lovers of their own selves, covetous, boasters, proud, blasphemers, disobedient to parents, unthankful, unholy, Without natural affection. . . despisers of those that are good, Traitors, heady, highminded, lovers of pleasures more than lovers of God. . . But evil men and seducers shall wax worse and worse, deceiving, and being

deceived." Christian, things are not going to get better, but worse the farther into the last days we enter.

4. Another **sign** is found in 1Timothy 4:1–3, "Now the Spirit speaketh expressly, that in the latter times some shall depart from the faith, giving heed to seducing spirits, and doctrines of devils; Speaking lies in hypocrisy; having their conscience seared with a hot iron; Forbidding to marry, and commanding to abstain from meats, which God hath created to be received with thanksgiving of them which believe and know the truth." The last days will be seen by the departure of the faith. There will be an immense falling away during the tribulation. However, it will begin even before. All we have to do is see the ministers, gospel singers, etc. who are renouncing the faith now.

5. Another **sign** is seen in Mark 13:4–5,13 that states, "Tell us, when shall these things be? And what shall be the sign when all these things shall be fulfilled? And Jesus answering them began to say, **TAKE HEED LEST ANY MAN DECEIVE YOU.** . . And ye shall be hated of all men for my name's sake: but he that shall endure (continue, persist, persevere, prevail) unto the end, the same shall be saved." Christian, expect to be hated, loathed, persecuted because you follow Christ. Pay attention to the fact that Jesus WARNS if we do not TAKE HEED, man will deceive us.

6. Another **sign** is found in Luke 21:25–28, "And there shall be signs in the sun, and in the moon, and in the stars; and upon the earth distress of nations, with perplexity; the sea and the waves roaring; Men's hearts failing them for fear; and for looking after those things which are coming on the earth: for the powers of heaven shall be shaken. And then shall they see the **Son of man coming in a cloud with power and great glory.** And when these begin to come to pass, then look up, and lift up your heads; for your redemption draweth nigh." Those who don't know Christ will have their heart fail, but God's soldiers will know these signs in the sun, moon, stars, and earth mean Jesus is about to return.

7. Another **sign** is John 6:40, where Jesus makes clear there will be no resurrection (emptying of graves) to everlasting life (raising up) until the last day.

8. Another **sign** is unmistakably clear in 2 Thessalonians 2:1–4. In those verses the Apostle Paul emphatically warns not to be deceived by any teaching that teaches our gathering together unto Christ (rapture) will happen **before** the falling away and the man of sin is revealed when he sits in the temple claiming to be God.

No where in the signs does it teach Jesus will pull us out before the tribulation. The opposite is quite clear. He is not returning until after the tribulation of those days where the sun shall be darkened, the moon shall not give her light, the stars shall fall from heaven, and the powers of the heavens shall be shaken. And then shall appear the sign of the Son of man in heaven. When the last trump sounds, the dead shall be raised incorruptible, and we shall be changed (1 Corinthians 15:52). Our gathering together unto Christ (rapture) will not take place until after the falling away and the man of sin sits in the temple claiming to be God.

Now, if we find ourselves here when the things in Revelation start to unfold, will it shake our foundation of faith? The apostle Paul and Jesus clearly warn us to not be deceived. Certain signs will happen before the gathering together to Christ (rapture) and Christs return. If we allow ourselves to be deceived through luke-warm Christianity's teaching, we will be overwhelmed. That's why there will be an incredible falling away from the faith like Esau who for one morsel of meat (the lust of his flesh) sold his birthright. Are we ready to go hungry? Are we ready to be slain for our faith? Have we been overcoming our fleshly desires in this life? If we haven't practiced self-denial here and now, how will we deny self when our life is on the line?

> Beloved, when I gave all diligence to write unto you of the common salvation, it was needful for me to write unto you, and exhort you that ye should earnestly contend for the faith which was once delivered unto the saints. For there are certain men crept in unawares, who were before

of old ordained to this condemnation, ungodly men, turning the grace of our God into lasciviousness, and denying the only Lord God, and our Lord Jesus Christ. I will therefore put you in remembrance, though ye once knew this, how that the Lord, having saved the people out of the land of Egypt, afterward destroyed them that believed not. . . Even as Sodom and Gomorrha, and the cities about them in like manner, giving themselves over to fornication, and going after strange flesh, are set forth for an example, suffering the vengeance of eternal fire (Jude 3–7).

We have moved so far away from the faith that once was delivered to the saints. I mean the kind of faith of the early Christians who endured such persecution. Today, God's soldiers are listening to the teachers Jude warned about. These ungodly men/women are preaching an ear tickling message that turns grace into a license for all sorts of sexual sins. Self-indulgence is taught which is a direct contradiction to the Scriptures teaching the necessity for self-denial of those who follow Jesus (Luke 9:23).

To help us further understand the rapture will not happen before the signs mentioned by Paul. Let me reiterate about the word "keep" in Revelation 3:10. The Greek word means "a watch, to guard from loss or injury. It implies a fortress, hold fast." It reveals a protection. We will be protected as the Israelites were in Goshen. They weren't taken out, but protected. God is our fortress (Psalms 91:2, Psalm 18:2). This Scripture does not imply we will be taken out, but kept or preserved during the time of temptation or adversity. In other words, we'll be enabled to keep the faith no matter what we may face.

This promise is only for those who have kept (held fast) the word of the Lord's patience. It means we have endured, prevailed, persevered, overcame. Listen to me, Paul makes emphatically clear in 2 Thessalonians 2:1–3 there will be NO gathering together or rapture before the signs of falling away and the man of sin sits in the Temple claiming to be God. To expect otherwise, is to be deceived and misinterpret the signs that are as clear as the handwriting on the wall.

Lord, please let the scales of deceit fall from our eyes and give us ears to hear what the Spirit has to say about the gathering together to Christ or the rapture. We're not promised we won't suffer plagues, hard times, tribulation, anti-Christ's persecution, etc.

The Early Church suffered severe persecution as revealed in my book, *Satan's Strategy to Torment through Physical Ambush: Educating God's Soldiers of Satan's Plot to Shatter Faith through Sickness and Disease.* We're only promised we won't suffer his wrath.

Wake up soldier, tribulation, trials, storms, obstacles, strategies of Satan, etc. are not God's wrath. The bowls of wrath in Revelation are NOT poured out until after the anti-Christ sits in the temple claiming to be God. Our gathering together (rapture) takes place after the falling away and the man of sin (the anti-Christ) sits in the temple claiming to be God. It's not time to be looking to get out of reality like the alcoholic, drug addict, etc. We are to be warriors of faith that stand in his armor, and are prepared through a knowledge of the word to take on the evil day!